CHASING

THE
MERRY-GO-ROUND

CHASING

THE
MERRY-GO-ROUND

A True Story

Holding on to Hope & Home
When the World Moves
Too Fast

KELLY BARGABOS

Boulay Press
San Diego, CA

CHASING THE MERRY-GO-ROUND
Holding on to Hope & Home When the World Moves Too Fast
A True Story

Publisher's Note: As a memoir, all incidents recounted herein are true
and accurate to the best recollection. However, for the sake of privacy,
some details, such as names and locations, have been changed.

Print License Agreement:

Alfred Publishing LLC
"Runaway Train"
Words and Music by David Pirner

Library of Congress Cataloging-in-Publication Data
Control Number: 1-5885936021

ISBN: 978-0-9994234-0-0 (paperback)
ISBN: 978-0-9994234-1-7 (ePub)
ISBN: 978-0-9994234-2-4 (mobi)

Designed by Gwyn Snider at GKS Creative
Edited by Christine Schmidt
Manufactured in the United States of America

www.kellybargabos.com

For Bobby

Home is a place all of us want to be. We all want to have our corner of the world, surrounded by people who know us, accept us, love us; a place where we are safe, warm, fed; a place where we have enough, where we are enough. This is all there is.

CONTENTS

AUTHOR'S NOTE

This memoir is a true story and is based on my own recollections and memories. My brother, Bobby, my parents, and my siblings provided valuable input as well. Every attempt was made to present this story as it actually happened. Excerpts from journals, personal letters, legal documents, and doctors' reports are authentic and presented as originally written. All the characters are real, though some names have been changed. I tried my best to tell the story of only Bobby and me. While there were and are many other critical and important characters, most of whom we are related to and love very much, I did not set out to tell their stories. I will leave that to them.

Chasing the Merry-Go-Round is about what life is like in a society that can move too fast for someone with intellectual and physical disabilities that are often invisible, especially at first glance. My heart has always been to tell the story of my brother, Bobby, so that people could see what life is truly like for someone like him.

I begin our story in 1976 when Bobby first entered my life. I tell his story mostly chronologically, but as you know, life is not always a neat, narrative arc that moves in a linear, chronological, and progressive path. Often and almost always, it is a series or set of messy circles that intersect and change and move and sometimes sit still for many years until one day something happens or someone says something at just the right time, in just the right way, and you suddenly see something clearly for the very first time in your life. You realize that something that happened to the six-year-old version of you is directly connected to your forty-year-old self, completing a circle that was in you all along and you had no idea. And so it was with me. I could not tell Bobby's story without telling at least some of mine.

This is how it really went down. I want to invite you, dear reader, to our corner of the world for an afternoon. I hope you read this story in the spirit it was written—to share my brother's story of struggle and hope, a simple soul who finds happiness and joy despite not getting the life he dreams of.

Thank you for reading our story.

PROLOGUE

I INCHED DOWN THE STREET TRYING TO FIND A HOUSE NUMBER on any of the homes with boarded-up windows that looked like they should be abandoned and condemned but actually had people living in them. Most of the homes on Munsell Street had numbers missing. This wasn't going to be easy. This was the last address I had for Bobby. It was 1993, and two years earlier he had left home at sixteen years old, long before sixteen-year-olds or anyone else had cell phones. He'd call me collect every few months and tell me where he was and what he was doing. I'd say, *Come home. I'll come get you. You can stay with me. You don't have to go back to school. You can get your GED, a job. Nobody's mad at you.* He wouldn't say much. The phone calls were fast. I took notes while he talked—streets, house numbers, people's names—information that would be useful on my next trip to Binghamton when I needed to find him.

This was also before GPS technology had replaced maps. I studied a map of Binghamton, a city in southern New York that sits near the border of Pennsylvania, and learned all the streets of the neighborhood he was usually in. If too much time went by between phone calls, I would drive to Binghamton and cruise Robinson Street or

Lyon Street or Front Street. I would pull my car up to people on the corner and ask if they knew Robert. I didn't have to give a last name or description; I could usually find him this way. He had a way of meeting people. Wherever Bobby has lived, his neighbors knew him. I found him on Thorpe Street once, on his birthday, when he was staying with someone named Sharon. I took him to eat at Friendly's and then to Kmart for some jeans, socks, T-shirts, and other things he needed, like a toothbrush and deodorant.

I pulled my car in front of a dark green three-story house. Two Doberman Pinschers were chained outside the second story window. They were pacing on top of the porch roof, which had obviously served as their toilet as well.

"I think this is it," I said.

"You're going in there?" my live-in boyfriend at the time, Kevin, asked as I opened the car door. "Kel. I don't think it's a good idea." He thought it was dangerous to walk up to a strange house in a strange neighborhood and start asking questions. He was probably right. Kevin readily accepted my relationship with Bobby and knew that I wouldn't stop until I found him. He had come to love Bobby too by then, and while he wasn't necessarily at ease with my plan that day, he did what he could to help me.

I got out of the car and walked up the sidewalk. The dogs on the roof pulled on their collars, barking. I wondered if the chains would hold. I saw faces in windows staring at me. Neighbors in their front yards watched. The dogs barked louder and louder the closer I got to the front door. I knocked and a skinny, old rat of a man answered.

"I'm looking for Robert. Bobby. He's my brother."

"He's not here."

"Do you know where he is? Where I can find him?"

"Nope. Haven't seen him for weeks."

I knocked on a few more doors but didn't find him that day. Kevin took over driving for the ride home from Binghamton while I shoved my Soul Asylum cassette into the tape player, turned it up, and choked out the words to their hit song at the time, "Runaway Train."

I stared out the window at a blurred slideshow of empty fields, billboards promising a different life if you shopped here or vacationed there, houses built before the highway came and bypassed them and left them to stand alone in their stubbornness, and I wondered if there was any hope for my brother. When the song finished, I rewound the tape and played it again. And again. The lyrics and aching melody of that song still take me back to those days of chasing and running, with Bobby always just beyond my reach.

The best way to describe what life is like for Bobby is an old-fashioned merry-go-round, like the one I grew up riding at the North Bay Elementary School playground. This merry-go-round was an octagon formed by wooden benches held together by steel bars radiating from the center pole. Metal grates covered the opening in the middle. Two hand-foot pumping stations, usually manned by fourth-grade boys, stood on opposite sides. They would push and pull on the steel bars, slowly at first, until they found their rhythm. Then they'd pump with as much speed as their feet and hands would allow. The rest of us held onto the wooden benches and ran in a pack. Our hands stung with splinters as we pushed as hard and fast as we could. Our sneakers pounded in unison, forming a deep rut in the hard dirt as we tried to keep up with the kids pushing, pulling, and setting the pace. If you faltered or lagged for even a moment, you lost your footing and risked falling. Kids that fell were stepped on. No one slowed down. There were no adults, no referees to guarantee fairness. It was every man for himself.

For Bobby, most of the time the world spins like this merry-go-round with the rest of us running in a pack at a pace he's not capable of. His brain is on cruise control, set at a speed that can't keep up with those who push and pull, make the rules, set the speed. The recorded voice when he calls Social Services or the gas and electric company, repeating option five, berates him to make a choice and threatens to hang up on him when he's still trying to figure out option one. The daily newspaper, job applications, forms for government assistance, and cell phone contracts—all geared for those with an eighth-grade education—are no match for his third-grade reading level. The bank teller who refuses to cash his paycheck because he doesn't have a checking account can't be bothered to take the time to listen to him explain why. The cashier at the grocery store rolls her eyes and sighs loudly when it takes him too long to count out his dollar bills and coins.

At the playground, once the merry-go-round reached top speed, we jumped onto the moving bench, clutched the bar in front of us, and leaned back into the wind. Silky, white milkweed seeds blew across our faces and got caught in our hair and mouths. Intoxicated with speed, we looked around at all the other kids who made it. We considered ourselves worthy of the ride and breathed a sigh of relief. Once on, you had to focus on your grip. You couldn't relax or look down at the kids who fell. If you did, you might be thrown off by the sheer force of the spinning, tossed three feet in the air to land on hard ground, maybe get the wind knocked out of you or a scraped knee or split lip depending on your landing.

Some kids knew they wouldn't be able to run fast enough. They saw the rut and the fate of those who tried and failed and decided to stand on the sidelines instead, watching. The rest of us laughed and screamed as if we were the only kids on earth, as if all that mattered to us was that we had a seat on the moving bench. We'd enjoy the ride as long as we could. Other kids couldn't bear to watch and not ride, so they'd walk to the other side of the playground to ride the swings, the teeter-totter, or the slide.

Most of the time, Bobby is one who stands on the sidelines and watches the rest of us go 'round. I tried for many years to help make him fast enough and strong enough to climb onto the merry-go-round. When that didn't work, I tried running for him. I tried carrying him while I ran. I was sure that if I could just get him up on that bench, he would be okay. Instead, he has shown me what it's like to stand on the sidelines.

And though I will always try to convince the ones pushing and pulling to slow down every once in a while—let people like him on or off, give someone else a turn—when he is on the sidelines, I will stand with him. When he walks to the other side of the playground, I will walk with him.

When I tell people my brother's story, our story, they always ask me *why*. Why did *I* take on the responsibility, the burden of my brother? Why am I so devoted to him? They ask these questions with their eyebrows raised, their puzzled faces pinched with judgment. Their next question is usually, "Where's your *mother*? Isn't this *her* job?" The truth is, my mother was there, still is. So is my father. My parents are the ones who rescued Bobby in the first place. They are the ones who fought for his life and didn't give up until he was safe, until there was no chance he would return to his biological parents. My mother raised him. She fed him, clothed him, got him to school, all the things a mother should do. My relationship with

Bobby wasn't created out of necessity or because my mother was deficient in her job.

My therapist, Dr. Marsha, had uncovered many years later that I had a considerable need to make sure those I loved were happy. She thought I learned at a very young age, when my family life was in turmoil, to be a good girl. She based this on a story I told her of a night I stood at the front door with my older sister, Shelly. It was very cold, and the icy air blew up the matching flannel nightgowns that my mother had made for us. It was a dark night and we should have been in bed, asleep. I suppose they thought we couldn't hear, but in our small one-story house, in the middle of the night, secrets were hard to keep. My mother was in the car in the driveway. My father stood at her window talking to her. I screamed. I cried. I begged her not to leave. I promised to be better. I promised to be good. The car stalled in the driveway. My father popped the hood to see if he could fix it. My mother eventually came back in the house.

I was pretty sure that scenes like this happened more than once in my first seven or eight years. I guess in that moment, and other moments like it, my fate was sealed. I would do whatever I could to keep my family together, to keep my mother happy, to keep her from leaving. To keep my home.

And so I was good. I cleared the table when it was my turn. I washed the dishes and did my homework. If I knew company was coming over, I would vacuum the pet hair off the couch and carpet. I would clean the bathroom, even when it wasn't my turn. I folded the clean laundry. My room was neat. I remember hoeing every row in our garden one afternoon in the hot sun while my brothers and sisters swam in the pool. I tried to keep my two sisters from killing each other. If I could keep peace in our home, then my entire world would not fall apart.

I was good at keeping the peace. I developed negotiation skills that could have been used to end world wars. One night, my parents were out and my older brother, Tim, who was twelve at the time, was babysitting the rest of us. Shelly was fighting with him, which wasn't unusual. He punched her; she punched him back. He pulled her hair; she dug her nails into his arm. He dragged her to the kitchen and pretended he was going to grab a knife out of the drawer. My younger sister, Patti, was five and hysterical, sobbing, and begging him not to stab Shelly. I knew he wasn't really going to get the knife. As I hugged Patti, trying to convince her that everything was going to be okay, I negotiated a truce between Tim and Shelly.

My world did not fall apart after all. My father stopped drinking; he didn't die. My mother got a little happier; she never left. My parents loved me. My sisters still fought and probably always would. Yet, I seemed convinced our family hung in a fragile state, real or imagined. I listened for slammed doors and raised voices. I didn't hide or run from them. I ran to them. Like how a barometer takes in atmospheric pressure and tells you whether or not a storm is coming, I could walk in a room and tell you who was unhappy, angry, depressed, or sad, and why. I absorbed other's feelings like a sponge. Over time, my family accepted my self-assigned role of keeper of peace, keeper of emotions, keeper of our home. So by the time Bobby came along, keeper of baby brothers was an obvious path for me.

I honestly don't know the answer to *why* when people ask me about my relationship with my brother. I don't feel like I need one, and I don't spend time thinking about it. All I know is that a baby showed up at my house one day, battered and bruised, needing someone to love him. And so I did.

PART ONE

SAVED

THE DAY
WE GOT BOBBY

I N MY FAMILY, AUGUST 10, 1976, HAS ALWAYS BEEN KNOWN as "the day we got Bobby." He was ten months old and I was eight. It was a day like any other except when I woke up that Tuesday morning, my father was home from work. I knew something was up. He usually left for the gravel pit while it was still dark outside. Most days, when I woke up before dawn and sleepily walked down the hallway to the one bathroom we all shared, I would see my mother hand him his black lunch pail; he would give her a kiss, say goodbye to the dog, and leave. We wouldn't see him again until seven o'clock that evening. My mother cooked dinner every night, and my brother and sisters and I had to wait until my father got home before we could eat. "How do you think your father feels?" my mother would ask as we sat on the front porch waiting for his pickup to pull in. We were convinced we would die if we didn't eat immediately. "He's been working all day in the hot sun," she said, unmoved by our whining. "You'll live."

But this day my dad was home. My parents announced that my two sisters and I were going to their friends' house for the day. My older brother didn't have to go; he and his best friend, Stephen, were joined at the hip, and he could stay at his place all day. They dropped us off that morning and didn't tell us where they were going, what they were doing, or what time they would be back. My little sister was convinced we were getting a new puppy. I was usually more of a worrier and so I wondered briefly if they were coming back at all. These friends of my parents had three daughters too, so before long, we were off to the playground and distracted from all the mystery of what my parents were up to.

That summer of '76 marked fourteen years that my parents had been married. Those years had not been easy ones. My dad's drinking had almost killed both of them and their marriage. His doctor told him that his thirty-five-year-old liver had cirrhosis so severe that one more drink of gin could kill him. He took another shot of gin, just to see if the doctor really knew what he was talking about, and landed in the hospital. I was six or seven years old, and my mother took all of us kids to visit him. They didn't let kids visit in patient rooms back then, so we waited downstairs. The nurse wheeled him into the waiting room, and we stood up so we could get a better look at him lying flat out on the stretcher. I don't remember what we said to him or if we talked at all. My father was a handsome man, with brown hair parted on the side that was usually neatly combed, blue eyes that crinkled when he smiled, a strong jaw and nose that fit just right on his face. That day in the waiting room, I wanted to memorize my father's face, as pale as the gown he wore, in case it was the last time I saw him.

He had survived that trip to the hospital, but they both knew time was running out for them. They hated each other, hated who they had become, both threatening to leave the other. But neither one ever did. Then one summer night in 1975 at a Methodist Church camp, they found God, or he found them.

⁓

Camp Aldersgate rested on a small lake in the woods. There was a dining hall, community room, and a small chapel set apart at the end of a grassy road. Cabins were spread across the property with names like Balsam, Spruce, and Hemlock nailed to the front door on wooden signs.

My parents thought this weekend retreat at the church camp would be a good idea for all of us, a different scene at least. We swam in the lake and played games in the woods. In the afternoon, families would square dance. At night, teenagers babysat the younger kids while the adults danced without us. At the center of the campground was a large pit. Grassy banks, sloped perfectly for theater-style seating, surrounded a circle of rocks that contained the campfire. There were always a few guitars and people to play them. We sang silly songs with funny voices and endless rounds of "Michael, Row the Boat Ashore" before moving on to the more serious songs. "Kum Ba Yah," the old spiritual that means come by here, was always the encore and no one left until all verses had been exhausted. *Someone's crying, Lord, Kum ba yah!* The youngest kids would fall asleep, their heads in the laps of an older brother, sister, or babysitter. *Someone's singing, Lord, Kum ba yah!* The dance had ended by now, parents came to stumble among us in the dark, finding their kids by the light of the fire. *Someone's praying, Lord, Kum ba yah!* And when the last verse was nearing the end, someone would shout out a new one they improvised. The end of the song signaled the end of the night, and no one wanted to leave the warm embrace of the golden-orange fire or the comfort of asking God to come by here. *Oh Lord, Kum ba yah!*

A guest speaker was scheduled for the service on Saturday night. My mother had arrived early to help Reverend Hicks with the set up. Her face relaxed and she moved quickly, happy to have something useful to do; she and my father had one of their worst fights ever in our cabin that morning. I don't know what they fought about. Maybe it was another bar tab that took his paycheck or the misery of pretending we belonged at this place with the other families, but he promised divorce for sure. My mother later told me that as they prepared for that night's special service, Reverend Hicks and my mother had discussed the guest speaker. There were rumors. Apparently he was part of a new trend, but getting *saved* was not something the Reverend was comfortable with. Reverend Hicks was not a fan of the "Jesus freak" movement and preferred to keep things traditional and more predictable.

"I don't want that Holy Spirit stuff anywhere near my service," he said.

"You would never catch me at this altar," my mother said.

When they were done, the room where we square danced the day before was lined with neat rows of folding chairs, a temporary altar and pulpit at the front.

I don't remember what the speaker said that night, but the service seemed to go on forever. I knew it was creeping past my bedtime, but I didn't care and I was determined to not look tired. I was going into third grade in the fall and felt I should be able to stay up later. My mom sat at the end of our row on the center aisle, my dad next to her. The four of us in order of age to the left. I was between my two sisters.

As the service came to an end, the speaker closed his Bible and walked to the front of the pulpit, looking out at the audience. He had a smooth face with kind eyes and a smile that made you trust him. Someone I couldn't see began to play the piano. We picked up our hymnals to find the right page as the crowd began to sing "Just as I Am." The room was still except for the soft, earnest singing and the speaker talking in the quietest voice he had used all evening. He paused in his speech, standing still at the front. Eyes open, eyes closed, looking at the crowd, looking up, like he was waiting for something.

A strange sound came out from my mother. I looked over. We all did. She was sobbing: shoulders up and down, gut in and out, tears and snot streaming down her beet-red face. When I looked again, her hymnal was on her chair, and she was at the front of the room, the first one at the altar. She told me later that she felt "someone" take the hymnal from her, place a hand on her shoulder, and guide her up the aisle. Other people left their seats and walked to the front of the room. Some of them began to kneel. Our mother continued to sob louder than anyone else. We looked to our right to see what our dad was doing, our eyes and faces shouting at him—go after her! She needs help! Can't you see she's crying? Other people in the room turned toward him, asking the same questions with their eyes. He didn't look at us. I'm sure he wanted to have one of his temper tantrums right there—pick up a folding chair and throw it, storm out, and slam the door. He was obviously annoyed at the spectacle my mother was creating. We waited, looking at him and each other, until he caved to the pressure. My mother told me later that when he met her at the altar he said, "You will pay for this. You have embarrassed me, and you will pay."

The truth is, something had to change soon or one or both of them would be dead, and the family they had tried to create would be destroyed. My father confessed many years later that one night he sat at a bar next to a young, dark-haired, olive-skinned guy he didn't know. My father was complaining about my mother and all her nagging. Nagging him to stop drinking, to come home at night, to stop spending all their money on booze. The dark-haired stranger offered to "take care" of his problem wife. Said he knew a guy. As my father considered the offer, his four young kids flashed through his mind, and he knew that solution was too extreme. He didn't know what to do, but he knew he couldn't do that.

So on that warm July night in 1975, my parents had nowhere else to go but to that altar. When the speaker asked if he could pray with them, they surrendered. We stayed in our seats and watched what was happening at the front of the room. The sky didn't open up. The ground didn't shake. There was no circle of light over their heads, and there was no voice from heaven telling us that everything was going to be okay. I wasn't sure at the time what it all meant but somehow knew that it was significant. The details of this scene are embedded deeper in my memory than my own first trip to the altar some months later. When they were done, my mother looked the same. My father left the altar, found a hiding spot outside by the fireplace, and smoked a cigarette.

After that night, my parents made new friends and attended Bible studies and church services. They began to hold hands again. Sometimes when we were riding in the car, their arms would stretch across the open space between their seats, their hands resting together on the console. I'm sure my parents felt like they were getting a second chance to get things right.

And on rainy Saturday afternoons, when my father got out of work early—normally a perfect day to hide from my mother and drink—he drove by his favorite gin mills, with pick-up trucks he recognized in the parking lot, and realized he hadn't thought about drinking since that night at the altar. He was able to keep on driving. He never drank again.

After that night, I didn't lie in my bed anymore and listen to the noise of a marriage shattering and wonder what it would be like if my mother moved out or my father took that last shot of gin. I didn't have to ask God to make it stop anymore. He already did.

It was almost one year after that night at the church camp when my mother's brother, George, called our house. My mother stood in our dining room, on our only phone, stretching out the long cord over the cereal bowls with leftover milk still on the counter. "Jeanne," he said to her, "do you think you and Carl could take Bobby?"

My mother once told me that she couldn't tell if he was sober when he called her that day. His thin voice seemed muffled, his words garbled by the phlegm in his throat. He lived in Binghamton, about two hours from our home. He had called my mother when his girlfriend, Ronnie, short for Veronica, became pregnant. They married after meeting with a priest who told them it was the only thing they could do about the pregnancy; they had no choice but to get married and have the baby. When my mother received the birth announcement with the picture of a ruddy, swollen newborn face with big, brown eyes, she wished she could have been excited or happy for her brother. Instead, the pit of her stomach filled with dread, and she wondered if he would be able to take care of a baby.

George hadn't been able to hold a job and relied on his monthly welfare check and food stamps. My mother had met Ronnie once or twice. She was short and thick with brown hair heavy with grease that hung perfectly flat to her shoulders from both sides of her middle part. She usually wore pants that were stained and dirty, hiked up above her waist with her flannel shirt tucked in tightly, buttons straining. She had a goofy grin revealing brown, uneven teeth. Rumor had it that Ronnie drank and dropped acid while she was pregnant, so my mother was relieved that the baby seemed healthy when he was born. George and Ronnie had been in and out of jail for petty things like loitering, pandering, or conning people out of their food stamps or disability checks. Once, George stole their older brother's social security card and license, using it to buy things on credit before he was caught. It took my uncle a long time to repair his credit history.

My mother asked George questions, trying to figure out what was going wrong, trying to figure out why he would ask them to take his son. I imagine the words she wanted to say were stuck in her throat. I'm sure she wanted to say: *What happened to you? Why can't you stop drinking and get a job? No. I can't take your baby. I have four kids now whom I can barely afford and no one to help me.*

We were finally growing up, and diapers and bottles were not something my mother longed for. My mother didn't recognize her brother anymore. The last time she saw him, with an unshaved face, his boyish buzz cut had grown into long, stringy hair. Showering was a rare occasion judging from the layer of dirt on his jeans and skin. He was four years older than her, yet he looked old enough to be her father. When they were young, she had helped him with his paper route. Her mother made her go with him on collection day because he couldn't count the change back to the customers. My mother couldn't remember when he started to drink. She thought it was after their parents' divorce, after their mom started drinking. He had dropped out of high school. She lost track of him when he became a carny.

With the phone still to her ear, I'm sure my mother looked at us lying on our bellies, hands holding up our heads in front of the television, still in our pajamas, with unbrushed hair and teeth. She told George she would have to talk to my dad. She knew it was only delaying the inevitable. The last thing he said to her before he hung up was, "I'm afraid Ronnie is going to kill him."

Every night after dinner my father showered off the layer of gravel pit he brought home with him. Usually he would come outside and play football or tag with us, but that night my parents went into their bedroom at the end of the hallway and closed the door. My mother told him about George's phone call. With four kids and more bills than paycheck at the end of every week, my parents wondered if bringing this baby home might disrupt their family. They had never discussed having more children. My mother was not one of those women who needed a new baby like a new purse or a new pair of shoes. And even though her brother felt like a stranger at times, she loved him and believed her nephew was in real danger. My dad told me he hesitated only because he worried they were taking the only child this couple would have. But he believed if the baby stayed with George and Ronnie, he would die from the abuse and neglect. My parents knew they didn't have a choice.

On August 9, six weeks after that phone call from George, Leonard Greene, the law guardian appointed by the county, called and asked my parents to come to Binghamton. A family court judge had ordered Bobby into the custody of Broome County Department of Social Services. They were removing him from George and Ronnie's home and asked if my parents were willing to take him. A county social worker, Susan Jay, had been working on this case for most of Bobby's short life. His doctor's office had reported many unexplained bruises around the face and a significant burn on the foot at four months. At one month, Bobby had been hospitalized with pneumonia. At two months, he was hospitalized again for a severe skin infection, impetigo. His doctor treated him for diaper rash so severe it was reported to the caseworker. He was fed spaghetti and meatballs instead of formula or baby food. He was served milk so hot he had burns on the inside of his mouth. His skin had been scalded in boiling hot baths and burned by cigarettes extinguished on his body.

The next day, after my parents dropped us off at their friends' house, they drove to Binghamton. First, to the courthouse to sign temporary custody papers. Next, Susan followed in her car as they drove to George and Ronnie's. They pulled up in front of a light green single-story rental. Animals and weather had ripped open trash bags left on the lawn instead of the curb for pick up. There were dogs milling around and endless piles of their waste in the yard.

Susan knocked and George opened the door to let them in. The smell of dog poop and baby diapers that had been left to rot wafted over them. My father said he recognized the smell of ammonia. He grew up on a farm and remembered the same smell from cow manure when he and his brothers had not cleaned the stalls completely. He usually had a strong stomach, but the combination of ammonia and garbage was fouler than anything he had ever encountered, even on the farm. He started to gag and knew he would vomit. He backed away from the door and waited outside. My mother followed Susan in the house.

Bobby was sitting in his playpen, his body covered with bruises, cigarette burns, and fleas. It wasn't just one or two fleas. It was the march of the fleas—crawling in and out of his ears, his nose, and the corner of his mouth. Susan tried to pack up some clothes for Bobby and any toys she could find while Ronnie cursed and screamed at them. My mother picked Bobby up, took him into the bedroom, and changed his days-old diaper. She saw that my father had walked around to the side of the house and waited outside the bedroom window. George stayed in the living room, silent, watching what was happening to his son. George knew he couldn't take care of him, my father later told me. Even though he was sad and disappointed, he knew.

"That's my baby," Ronnie screamed. "You're not going to take him."

Ronnie kept screaming, "That's my baby. You can't take him." She pleaded with Susan, promising to keep Bobby in the playpen all the time so he wouldn't get hurt anymore.

My mother opened the bedroom window from inside, and the smell pierced my dad's nose again. He gagged. My mother handed Bobby through the open window to my father.

They took two brown paper bags of Bobby's clothes and a white bouncy seat, got in their van, and drove away. The two bags were filled with bloodstained clothes that had holes from cigarette burns and were infested with fleas. They had to be destroyed shortly after we brought them home, and our house had to be fumigated.

Bobby didn't make a sound and stayed quiet for the two-hour ride. He lay on the floor of the van between the two front seats and looked up at my parents. His brown eyes betrayed the sadness of his short life. My father later told me he was convinced that Bobby looked relieved.

Eight hours after they had mysteriously dropped us off at their friends' house, my parents pulled into their driveway in our '76 Chevy van. My sisters and I ran over to see what they had to say for themselves and to see if there was, in fact, a new puppy. As my parents got out of the van, exhausted, the adults looked at each other with eyebrows raised and wide eyes thinking that we didn't notice. I could tell they wished we weren't there so they could really talk. My sisters and I were quiet, suddenly uneasy with the surprise. My dad pulled the handle on the side of the van and the wide door rolled back. And then I saw something I hadn't imagined. On a blanket between the two front seats of the van, sleeping soundly on his belly, was a baby boy—thumb in his mouth, soft blond hair, upturned nose. Sweet and beautiful. For me, it was love at first sight.

…panic

THE WAITING ROOM OUTSIDE DR. MARSHA'S OFFICE was small. There were exactly two chairs surrounded by three-foot-high bookshelves. It was distinctly quiet except for the silver boom box, like the one I had in the eighties, set on top of the bookshelves playing soft jazz music. I assumed this was so we wouldn't hear her conversation with the client before us. I flipped through a magazine with my hands while my eyes and mind wandered around the room.

Dr. Marsha opened her office door. Kevin and I looked up and then quickly looked away. The space was tight and it felt intrusive to look at the woman coming out of her office. Was she here for the same reason I was? Or maybe she was an alcoholic. Maybe she'd been abused as a child. Or perhaps something worse. Out of politeness, I pretended not to see her. For the first time in my life, I understood the shame of such desperation and pain. I didn't want to look in her eyes because I was afraid I'd see me.

Dr. Marsha sent the woman on her way and then peered around the corner. "Are you Kevin and Kelly?" she asked.

We both stood up while avoiding direct eye contact with each other. I hadn't seen Kevin in a week.

"Yes," I said.

"Please come in."

Her desk and files were to the right as you entered her office. The left side looked like a living room without the television. Two loveseat-sized sofas were set opposite each other with a single armchair at one end. This was her chair. There was a small digital clock that sat on a table opposite from Dr. Marsha. I was relieved to have the clock there. At one hundred dollars an hour, I wanted to make sure we got our money's worth. Kevin sat on the plaid, over-stuffed sofa, and I sat on the low, black, leather one, across from each other, still avoiding eye contact.

Dr. Marsha held a blank yellow legal pad and a pen. She looked at us silently while we waited for her to start. We didn't know how to do this. Kevin held a half-empty water bottle in his hands. The plastic buckled and popped while he unscrewed the cap and then screwed it back on, over and over again. Therapy was new for both of us. Dr. Marsha had the same piercing eyes as my first piano teacher, my 4-H sewing teacher, the librarian at school, people whose looks always held many pointed questions and made you squirm in your seat. Her hair was blonde and curly, cut in a bob style; her nose was thin and petite. She reminded me of a delicate, pretty bird. She wore dark dress pants with short black boots and an expensive leather blazer. Her head pointed down so her blue eyes could see us over her glasses.

"Why are we here?" she asked.

"I had an affair," Kevin said. Yes, this is why we couldn't look at each other. He unscrewed the cap of his bottle again and took a sip of water. I began to cry and reached for a tissue from the box that was on the table with the clock.

"Tell me what happened."

We spent the remainder of those sixty minutes, and many more sessions after that, doing our best to describe what had become of us.

I began with the day that panic punched me in the chest. For the first time in my life, I knew true panic. The kind where your heart pounds as if it's going to explode through your skin, your mind races, and your palms sweat. You instantly feel like you could throw up everything you've ever eaten. You start looking around for a way to escape it. I had felt moments of panic before. Like the time when I was little and I thought my dad was dying in the hospital but then he didn't, or the day I thought I lost my five-year-old nephew at a crowded beach but found him three minutes later. Or when we found out the lump in my mother's breast was cancer. And the time I watched my father almost drown on the last day of our vacation in Ocean City, Maryland. But those moments of panic were different. They were short-lived with happy endings. I was talking about the kind of panic that is real and won't go away. There is no happy ending because the very thing you feared most has happened, and there is no going back.

I had been married for 12 years. On that particular morning, it was 11 years and 346 days. I had been with this man for 18 years and 323 days. We had a pretty good run of it. We loved each other and were best friends; we traveled, partied, and genuinely enjoyed each other's company. At times we disagreed and occasionally had fights, but I had always thought we had a special relationship, a love that was different. When I looked at our friends and other couples we knew, I believed we were ahead of the game. I was wrong.

Months before, I had started to feel things shift in our relationship. Looking back, I can point to a few specific times I knew something was wrong. There were whispers I pretended not to hear. I felt it when we had sex. There was an unfamiliar tension between our naked bodies. I watched him behave like an unfamiliar person—drinking too much, picking fights with me over the way I looked at him when I said goodnight, or for changing the channel at the wrong time—acting like a man I'd never seen in our eighteen years together, making strange comments to me like, "Do you think we're going to make it?"

But we carried on with our life. That spring, we went with friends to a Meatloaf concert. We took a long weekend trip to New York City in April and rowed a boat around the lake in Central Park, had brunch at the Boathouse, spotted celebrities, and had a candlelit dinner on the sidewalk in Little Italy. In May, we spent two luxurious days at a spa close to our home. We relaxed and pampered ourselves with massages and pedicures and long dinners spent talking about us. The whispers were still there.

One or two days after the spa weekend, I happened to hit the back button on our computer and discovered that he had an email account I had never seen before. The whispers were now voices.

The next morning, Kevin left early to take Bobby to an appointment with his job coach, who was helping thirty-two-year-old Bobby find a job that was suited to his skills. I logged on to the computer and went to this new email site I had stumbled upon. I tried all of the passwords I knew Kevin had used and none of them worked. And then, with my fingers poised over the keyboard, my mind spinning, a name came to me and I typed it in.

The password worked and I suddenly found myself in his inbox, surprised it was that easy. Subject lines of emails shouted at me. I knew in an instant. *Oh my God. He's in love with someone else. He wants to leave me. I was right. It was her. Oh my God, they've had sex! Many times.* I opened a few emails and printed two or three. I managed to focus my mind long enough to forward the emails to my address. I knew he would delete the evidence as soon as I confronted him. My stomach hurt. My heart pounded. My mind raced. I needed to get out of there. He would be home any minute, and I knew I couldn't see him. I also knew I needed to leave right away so that I wouldn't be late to work. I shut down the email and ran to my closet. I grabbed a black leather weekend bag with the gold logo from my previous company on the side. *What do you pack when you leave your husband?* I couldn't focus my thoughts. I managed to randomly grab two pairs of underwear, a pair of jeans, and a T-shirt. My mind was unable to think in complete sentences. I zipped the bag, grabbed the emails I had printed, and ran out of the house to my car. I held my breath until I was out of our neighborhood and knew I was safe from seeing him.

My whole body shook as I made the thirty-minute drive to work. I reminded myself to keep breathing while I tried to think about what I should do next. I wondered if my marriage was over. I wondered if he would leave me and never come back. How could the same man who had been by my side as I chased after Bobby for the last eighteen years, the same man who helped me move my brother in and out of at least fifteen different apartments, and drove him to doctor appointments, to the grocery store, did anything I asked of him to help with my brother, how could this kind and generous man be capable of so much hurt? I wondered how we could ever be in the same room again. *What would become of my home?*

THE FIGHT
TO KEEP HIM

RONNIE CALLED OUR HOUSE A LOT IN THOSE FIRST few weeks after we brought Bobby home. My mother accepted her collect calls and listened to her say, "Robert's my baby, Jeanne. He's not your baby. His ma loves him." My mother would let her talk until she grew tired of repeating herself. She didn't respond to Ronnie's accusations or enter into conversation but tried to answer her questions as directly as possible. My mother had already learned that Ronnie would twist her words and lie, telling the caseworker my mother was trying to steal her baby and refusing to let her see him again.

Having a baby in our home with diapers and bottles didn't seem to cause chaos. Bobby needed love and safety and nourishment from us, and at the same time, didn't need us at all. He didn't cry for attention. He didn't manipulate or ask for things. He could sit or lie down for hours without anyone paying attention to him and it wouldn't bother him.

My mother began keeping notes like these in her journal so that she could update the caseworker, Susan Jay, with letters and phone calls.

November 22, 1976

A lot sure has happened since we brought him home. George and Ronnie have been up once since that time in August. She called me every night for about three weeks. Did not pay for all calls either. What a mess. She ended up in jail for a couple of days in October due to some stunt she pulled. They didn't even acknowledge Bobby's birthday on September 22. He's almost fifteen months now. What a change in him. You wouldn't know it was the same baby, he crawls all through the house, says quite a few things. See, Bye-bye, Ma, Da-da. He can do patty-cake. He's not so full of fear as he was. Has cut a lot of teeth.

Susan Jay was up today for a couple of hours, going over things. George and Ronnie have been to court about three times. The last time was August 17 and Bobby was to stay in the custody of Broome County for eighteen months. Which means we'll have him for that long.

My mother also sent a picture of Bobby to the caseworker after he had gained a few pounds and grew a couple of inches. She reported that he loved to eat peanut butter and jelly sandwiches and soup. "A good baby even when cutting teeth."

Ronnie became the one to look out for. Back then, there was no such thing as caller ID, and picking up the ringing phone was a game of roulette. You never knew who was on the other end. This alone made for excitement in our house, and it was always a contest to see who could race to the phone first and be the one to answer. One night while my parents were at Bible study, I happened to get to the phone first. It was Ronnie. She did most of the talking as I tried to work into the conversation that my parents weren't home and she'd have to call back. She wanted me to tell my mother that George had a job now and they'd be up soon to get Bobby back.

November 30, 1976
Bobby started walking on the nineteenth, but then he got sick
for a week with a terrible sore throat, so he kind of backed
off.

That winter, Bobby became very sick one night, so I cradled him in my nine-year-old arms. I couldn't stand the thought of him not being okay. I sat in our living room, holding him in his blue sleeper pajamas with my arm resting on the arm of the couch. The television was on but turned down low while we waited for my dad to get home from work so we could eat dinner.

"Kelly, he's fine. Go put him in his crib. He just needs to sleep," my mother told me.

"It's okay. I can hold him," I said. I couldn't put him down. Even then, I thought I knew better. I insisted on holding him while he slept and slept and slept. I saw the headlights from my dad's truck light up our big picture window. Our Saint Bernard, Barfy, started to bark.

"Dad's home," my mother announced. "Let's get ready for dinner."

"I'm not hungry," I said.

"You are going to sit at the table and eat." I could tell by her tone that I was going to lose this battle. Reluctantly, I laid Bobby down on the chair that was closest to the dining room. This chair was one of our newer pieces of furniture, with a pattern of big orange, blue, and brown flowers, and it swiveled. I turned the chair toward the dining room. Luckily, my seat at the table was close to the living room, so I could keep an eye on him while I swallowed my dinner as fast as possible. I scooped him up again and held him for hours that night while he slept with his hot, fevered skin next to mine. I wouldn't get up to go to the bathroom or even when I lost all feeling in my arm because I knew my sister would grab him if I did. I was holding Bobby, but it felt like he was holding me.

Christmas Day 1976
We had to go to Syracuse to pick up George and Ronnie at the bus station because Mom was so drunk. They drank when they got up here. They stayed here for an hour. Did they ever stink. Brought a lot of presents for Bobby—card, snowsuit, jacket, slippers, shoes, two outfits, and socks. They came down again Sunday on their way back. Bobby has not been the same since they were here. Very fearful. Still remembers, I think.

George and Ronnie had called my grandmother on Christmas Eve to announce they were coming up. I think they felt like they had an ally in my grandmother. She had a bad habit of getting drunk at inappropriate times, like every day, which was unfortunate because my mother could have used her help. Whenever George and Ronnie made the bus trip north to Syracuse, New York to visit Bobby at our house, they stayed overnight with my grandmother who, of course, liked the drinking company.

December 28, 1976

Dear Mrs. Jay,

Thought I'd drop you a few lines to let you know how things are going. Bobby's parents were up in November. Ronnie showed no interest in Bobby at all. She didn't even pick him up. They called my mother Christmas Eve and said they were coming up the following day. As it turned out, my mother couldn't go get them, so we drove to Syracuse to get them (only because it was Christmas Day.) They bought Bobby some nice things, which he needed, but she also upset him quite a bit. He has not been the same for a week now. He went back to how he was when we got him. He has just sat around, no smiling, talking, or eating. He hasn't been sleeping either. He seems to be full of fear just like when we got him.

Ronnie said she was getting him back soon and that she was going to keep him in the playpen at all times, even to sleep so as not to get in trouble. George also told my mother that he thought Bobby remembers when Ronnie beat on him and threw him up against the wall.

Before all of this, Bobby was doing very well. He has been walking about three weeks now. All over the house and was eating well and gained about three more pounds. He's still cutting teeth. He has lost a couple of pounds this week.

Sincerely,
Mrs. Bargabos

Sunday, January 16, 1977
Ronnie called. Said she wanted her son back.

It took ten months for the judge to be satisfied with the reports from Susan before the county officially approved my parents as foster parents. My parents and Susan continued to push the courts for permanent custody. Susan came to our home several times for official inspections. She was about the same age as my mother, tall and slender with brown hair and glasses, and always smiling. She would spend a few hours each visit, sometimes having lunch or dinner with us. Susan was able to see that when Bobby joined our family of six, he dethroned my little sister, Patti, as the baby of the family. He went from abuse and neglect to three older sisters fighting for the right to hold, change, and feed him.

Susan walked through our house to see where he was bathed, fed, and where he slept. The first night he was with us, my mother gave Bobby a bath while my sisters and I hung over her shoulders, elbowing each other, fighting to be the one to hand her the shampoo or the towel. She filled the tub with lukewarm water and lowered him into the bath. He stretched his legs out straight in front of him, screaming, trying to keep his toes from touching the water. She would repeat this every night for a few weeks until he was convinced that she wouldn't burn him with bath water. After his bath that first night, with a clean diaper and no fleas, my mother laid him in a crib in her bedroom. In the middle of the night, a few hours after he had fallen asleep, he screamed suddenly, piercing the darkness. My father shot out of bed and picked him up. He prayed softly in his ear until he stopped screaming before he settled him back into his crib. His crib stayed in my parents' bedroom for more than a year. He never screamed like that again.

March 1977
Bobby started to whistle when he was about eighteen months
old. He sure is a busy little guy. Seems to be quite smart and
alert.

Bobby was put down to bed before the rest of us, and one night we heard this lovely, strange sound coming from his crib. At eighteen months old, he had taught himself to whistle. I was amazed. I had always wanted my father to teach me. I think he tried, but I could just never get the hang of a real, easy whistle. I could only get a whistling sound if I drew my breath in sharply—the note came on the intake, instead of the out, like it was supposed to. My dad was a master at it. He would serenade us with whole melodies and folk songs while he did other things—mow the lawn, shave, or walk around the house. And now Bobby had taught himself to do it. From that night on, Bobby whistled in his crib until he fell asleep. In the mornings, when he woke earlier than the rest of us, his melody woke us up. I'm not sure where his songs came from; they must have been hidden in him somewhere.

December 14, 1977

Dear Mrs. Bargabos:

We are proceeding slowly in court. An initial hearing should
be scheduled some time in late January. My best to you and
your family over the holidays and a hug to the little one!
What a beautiful picture he took—I could see the twinkle in
his eye!

Susan Jay

George and Ronnie continued to visit every so often, and none of us liked it. My sisters and I hovered around them like the yellow-shirted security teams do at a concert or basketball game, arms crossed, with their back to the action in order to keep their eyes narrowed on the crowd, looking for any wrong move, ready to protect spectators from bad guys at a moment's notice. We prowled around the living room, pretending to be watching television, if they were visiting on the couch. If they sat in a circle of lawn chairs in the front yard, we rode our bikes in the driveway. If they sat at the picnic table, we chased our dog around the backyard. We never took our eyes off them or Bobby.

Their last visit was when Bobby was almost two. George and Ronnie had come up from Binghamton during the week to visit, so my father was probably at the gravel pit. Ronnie sat at our dining room table with Bobby stiff in her lap. George sat a few chairs down, closer to the set of double windows that looked out into the backyard. The sun warmed the grass and the sand pile, where Bobby would have been playing with the dog or his trucks if they hadn't come to visit. My sister, Shelly, who was ten or eleven at the time, sat across from Ronnie so she could keep an eye on her. I sat by my mother. My mother made small talk with George about the weather or what she was making for dinner, maybe about my grandmother's latest antics. While they were talking, Ronnie looked across the table, straight into Shelly's eyes, giggling and laughing, took her cigarette, and butted it out on Bobby's forearm. He screamed while she used his arm like an ashtray.

"What do you think you're doing?" my mother cried. She jumped up and ran around the table. She yanked Bobby out of her arms. I didn't know what to do. I had been focusing on the conversation between my mother and George and didn't see it coming. I don't

remember George saying anything at all or making a move to protect Bobby.

"Get out!" my mother told them. "Get out of my house."

Shelly was frozen in her seat, unable to take her eyes off Ronnie's
face and the grin that stayed there minutes after my mother yelled
and took Bobby out of her arms. That grin would be seared into my
sister's memory. She told me that whenever she thinks of that day
and that grin, chills still move up and down her spine. That was the
last time George and Ronnie were allowed to visit.

HOME FOR NOW

March 8, 1978

Dear Mrs. Bargabos,

We have a court hearing scheduled for 3/16/78—I will try to call you after the hearing. It's only a preliminary hearing, so little will be accomplished. I have spoken to Bobby's law guardian and he seems pretty neutral about the permanent custody. He is reading my folder and maybe will be swayed by that.
Give Bobby a hug for me!

Thanks-
Sue Jay

My parents tried everything they could think of to keep Bobby, hoping that the courts would rule in their favor. They prayed a lot back then, about everything, but Bobby was at the top of the list. They prayed for George and Ronnie too, but mostly that Bobby would never go back. He was on the prayer list at church. They recruited friends and their pastor, who had witnessed our family embracing Bobby, to write letters of recommendation, vouching for their character and integrity.

June 26, 1979

Mrs. Lila Shole
Supervisor, Foster and Adoptive Homefinding
Children's Division
Department of Social Services

Dear Mrs. Shole:

Thank you for giving me the privilege to recommend Mr. and Mrs. Carl Bargabos as an adoptive family. I have known the Bargabos family since 1975, and I have found them to be a fine Christian family of good moral character. Both Mr. and Mrs. Bargabos are excellent parents, and I would highly recommend them as adoptive parents. If I can be of any further assistance please feel free to contact me.

Sincerely in Christ Jesus,

H.G. Cunningham
St. Hubert's of the Lakes

My mother later told me about one of the final court sessions when she was called to testify. The county courtroom was small and unremarkable, all wood and pale walls it seemed, except for the American flag and the state flag stationed on either side of the bench. She held her hands tight in her lap so the lawyer and the judge couldn't see them shaking. My father sat in the chairs with a friend while the lawyer assigned to represent Bobby drilled my mother with questions for more than an hour.

"Mrs. Bargabos, can you explain why Bobby appears to be pudgy? I see it runs in your family; what exactly are you feeding him?"

"Mrs. Bargabos, is it true that you've never liked Ronnie and just want to steal her baby?"

"Mrs. Bargabos, Ronnie has told the court you refused to let her see Bobby? Why?"

"Mrs. Bargabos, you have four children of your own. Can you tell the court why you want to take away your brother's only son?"

My mother answered his questions and tried not to let the lawyer rattle her. Her brother was there, but not Ronnie. She couldn't tell if he was mad or sad. He just sat in his chair and looked straight ahead. He didn't say anything. He didn't give any testimony. Maybe he was relieved. He was the one who called my mother in the first place and asked her to take him. Maybe he knew it was the right thing.

On August 13, 1979, my parents appeared in front of the judge again. We snapped a picture that day. Bobby stood in front of my sisters, my older brother, and me; we made a half circle behind him. Tim, the oldest, had a hand on his shoulder. We stayed behind the table when my parents moved in front of the bench.

"The child's time living with the birth parents is well-documented as to an infant's malnourishment and maltreatment. The parental rights are terminated due to the parents' inability to care for a baby regardless of all interventions."

After three years of fighting for Bobby's life, my parents were granted the petition of adoption. Bobby had settled into our family long before the judge made it official. Still, it was a relief to have it done. I thought then that the rescue effort was complete but wouldn't know for many years to come that we still had a long way to go.

But for now, he was home.

...a place to start

DR. MARSHA'S WAITING ROOM WAS EMPTY AND quiet except for the soft jazz music coming from the boom box. I took a seat and checked my watch. I'd arrived with a few minutes to spare. It was always a race to get there on time. I waited until the last possible second to leave my office. It was a twenty-minute drive on a country road to get to Dr. Marsha and then an hour session with her. This had me out of the office for almost two hours. I always tried to schedule my appointments around noon so I could pretend I was taking a late lunch and scoot in and out of my office without being noticed. I hadn't told my coworkers or my boss where I was really going or what had happened in my marriage. Kevin is the one who called my sister and parents and told them what had happened. I was embarrassed and ashamed and didn't want anyone to know that I was not enough for my husband.

Missing work was not my style; as chief financial officer of my company, I had a lot of responsibility and stress. I liked going to work and let the problems and challenges of my workday push aside what was happening with my husband, or the latest crisis with

Bobby as I fought to get him seen and heard by his doctors and others we needed help from. At least for eight or ten hours, I could avoid what was happening in my personal life.

Although Kevin and I would continue with our joint sessions, Dr. Marsha believed that before we could answer the questions about whether or not our marriage could be salvaged, we needed individual sessions to work on "family of origin" issues. Kevin had already started his solo sessions. He had a lot to work on. His childhood was complicated and intense; it had a tremendous impact on the man he had become. However, that is not my story to tell. I was convinced I did not have any significant family of origin issues. I knew my family wasn't perfect; no family is. But I thought ours was fine. As Dr. Marsha had explained to us in our previous session, "Kevin, your childhood and the things that happened to you are like front page news. Kelly, you had some issues too that helped shape and define who you are, but yours are more like page six."

Dr. Marsha opened her office door right on time and ushered out a couple. I looked down at my magazine until they passed.

"Kelly, come on in," she said.

I took a seat in my usual spot—the middle of the black leather couch, feet scooped up under me, hugging a pillow in my lap. I moved the tissue box closer to me. Dr. Marsha sat tall in her armchair with her blank yellow legal pad and pen held at attention.

"Where would you like to start?" she asked, pointing her eyes at me over the rim of her glasses.

I shifted uncomfortably in my seat, then shifted my feet out from under me and planted them on the floor. I set the pillow down and quickly picked it up again. I didn't know how to answer Dr. Marsha. I was uncomfortable with the anger that I usually kept on lockdown. Anytime it began to bubble to the surface, I quickly refocused my attention. I did not allow myself to feel that kind of emotion, especially when it was about me. But if I did express it, I'm pretty sure my anger at Kevin would sound something like this:

I'm angry that last Christmas we sat next to her at your office party, and I knew something was different. I felt it. I asked you about it, and you denied that anything was going on. But I knew. I'm angry that you complained we had no passion anymore and blamed me. I'm angry that after the first time you two slept together in February, you took me to Florida two days later and slept with me. How could you? How dare you! I'm pissed that for three months you kept it up while I knew our life was falling apart. I asked you what was wrong over and over again, and the whole time you were writing her lust-filled emails. I couldn't get you to tell me a single feeling or thought in your head and yet you sent her all kinds of professions of love and how she completes you and how beautiful she is—blah, blah, blah! Fuck you! I'm angry that it's her face I see when you and I have sex. I'm angry that songs on the radio remind me of you and her. I'm angry that our friends and family know. You kept going and going until you were caught red-handed and couldn't get away with it anymore. Then you had a breakdown. You lost your job because of her. I'm angry that you lied to me when you lost your job and that I had foolishly believed you. I'm angry that you're depressed and have anxiety, and I'm angry at whatever happened in your childhood to make you this way. I'm angry that you sat next to me in church every Sunday and it didn't convince you to do the right thing. I'm angry with God that my prayers didn't protect our marriage. Most of all, I'm angry that you made me believe that all of this was my fault.

Anger was exhausting.

On the other side of this anger was intense sadness, a feeling that left me confused and scattered. I wondered why we don't get bereavement time for a marriage when it dies. All those years suddenly gone. I can get time off for losing a parent or sibling, which makes sense. But I would also get a week to recover for my uncle, who I've seen maybe ten or twenty times in my entire life, but nothing for the man to whom I gave my life? The man I gave my heart, my soul, my youth? What about that loss? Don't I deserve a week to stay in bed and not get up?

I daydreamed about tombstones for marriages that had died and what the epitaphs might read. Perhaps, "The 'worse' got the best of them," or "They didn't forsake all others," or maybe it could read, "They had a good run." What would the end date be? When was it pronounced dead? Would it be the date of the divorce? The date one of them moved out? Would it be the first date he betrayed me? Or would it be the day I discovered the affair, May 8, 2007? The day I started to die. The day my life was forever changed and the light inside snuffed out. I settled on what I thought our tombstone could read—"Kelly and Kevin: they were happy once."

Didn't Dr. Marsha know that everything was different now? Everything I thought I knew, everything I thought I had figured out, wasn't true anymore. Didn't she know that it changes you in ways you don't expect, like buying birthday or Christmas cards? I'd stand in the aisle reading those meant for a husband and burst into tears when I realized that the sentiment expressed by Hallmark wasn't true for me anymore.

Should I start by telling Dr. Marsha that even after the anger and sadness I was unable to express were sufficiently trapped in the chasm of my chest, never to come up for air or to see the light of day, that there was this intense longing that bewildered me? There were nights I was pulled so strongly toward my closet, of all things. I wanted to take my pillow and a blanket into my carpeted walk-in closet, close the door, and curl up on the floor. I can't tell you why, but I wanted it badly.

There were days when I physically craved, like you would a cigarette or a shot of whiskey, being at my mother's house, curled up on her couch, with an afghan over me, and her placing a cool hand on my forehead and walking away clicking her tongue and getting me some ginger ale and saltine crackers. I wanted to sleep in my parents' house again. I wanted to curl up with my mother and have her hug me.

But I didn't tell Dr. Marsha any of that. I had spent all my life up to that point making sure that everyone else around me was okay, trying to keep all the balls in the air. What would happen if I were honest with my anger and sadness and longing? I didn't have the guts to find out. Not that day.

I looked around Dr. Marsha's office, searching for something to say that could explain what I was avoiding. Instead, I shrugged and raised my hands, palms up. I looked at Dr. Marsha and then away. *Where would I like to start, indeed?*

EASY

BOBBY PUT ONE KNEE UP OVER THE EDGE AND grunted until he was flat on his belly. He used his arms to get up on all fours and then stood up on our shaky coffee table. He picked up my dad's oversized Bible with the hand-stitched leather cover, struggling to keep it in his four-year-old arms.

"Pastor Bates say no fight? No fight!" He pointed one finger up in the air for emphasis, like our pastor did on Sunday mornings. "Amen? Amen."

"Pastor Bates say I yuh you? I yuh you!" He pointed one finger at a page in the open Bible. "Amen? Amen."

The violence of his early life had not seeped into Bobby's heart. He didn't like fighting, especially between his brother and sisters. This was something Bobby and I had in common. I imagined there was a part of him that remembered the yelling and anger that surrounded him in his first ten months of life. Even though it was usually normal sibling unrest and fighting over what to watch on TV or who had dibs for the telephone, I was unsettled by it too. My self-assigned role as peacekeeper kept me busy, but my strategy was to negotiate and talk whoever needed it out of their feelings. Bobby's strategy was to preach. We were in church every Sunday and sometimes attended services during the week.

When he was done admonishing his brother and sisters to stop fighting and love each other, he set the Bible down on the table and sang with certainty, "Jesus Loves Me," each word anchoring his faith and those of us within earshot. "Yeh, yeyuh yuh me, yeh, yeyuh yuh me...."

As he learned to talk, Bobby struggled with proper speech, and his own unique language developed. He would walk in the living room where I was watching television. "Wha you ben doey?" he'd ask. "Nothing, what're you doing?" I'd reply.

"Nutty mut," he answered. If my mother asked him what he wanted for lunch, he might say, "I nee no." Or ask for another "peanee boyee" sandwich. We latched on to the way he spoke, talking to each other the way Bobby would talk to us. I don't think his impaired speech alarmed any of us at the time; instead, it became the secret language of my family, which probably didn't help Bobby's speech development. He started kindergarten on schedule and right away was classified as severe speech/language impaired with average-to-low abilities. His elementary school didn't find his special language quite as endearing as we did, and after years of speech therapy he spoke like the rest of us, more or less.

Bobby made the journey from toddler to little boy to boy look easy. He was easygoing, even tempered, and eager to please; he was happiest watching *The Dukes of Hazzard* and *Knight Rider*, playing with his collection of Matchbox cars on the living room floor, and of course, eating peanut butter and jelly sandwiches, ice cream, or buttered popcorn. We didn't realize then that these would be the easiest years of all, and that life with Bobby would get much harder.

That my parents would someday say things like, "He was such an easy kid, never had to spank him like I did you other kids," or "He was always so good, would play for hours by himself." Even I would find myself looking back and trying to figure out how things could go so wrong when they seemed to start out so right.

My mother loved to send us outside "to air our fannies out." She led us to believe she had locked the door to keep us from coming in the house too soon. It wasn't so bad in the summer. Our house sat on an acre of land, which seemed as big as it sounds. We lived on a busy road, and when we weren't riding bikes in the driveway or posing in the ditch as cars passed by or pumping our arm in the air to get the eighteen-wheelers to honk their horn, we were in the backyard. The backyard was big enough for a four or five row, industrial-sized clothesline, a small shed with a sand pile behind it, a vegetable garden, and an aboveground pool. This still left a football field in the far back against the woods, which is where the ball games took place.

It took Bobby a long time to master throwing the baseball or football and riding a bike. He finally conquered the two-wheeler when he was about eight or nine years old. But swimming came easy to him. After my mother got the brown-green algae water from the fire department loaded with enough chemicals to clear it out so we could see the blue bottom, we would swim every day, all day for the rest of the summer. We'd walk in a circle in the same direction to try and get a whirlpool going, take turns shouting sentences to each other under water to see if the other person could make out what you were saying, race each other from end to end, have gliding contests, do somersaults, and whatever outrageous, goofy pose we could come up with while jumping off the side.

We taught Bobby how to swim. With his bubble belt, he could lap the pool, jump off the side, and ride on our backs playing horsey or shark all day. While the rest of us were fair-skinned, freckled, and burned easily, the sun turned his sandy hair a paler shade and his skin browned evenly.

Winter days—kicked out of the house—called for snowsuits, boots with bread-bag liners, and handmade mittens and scarves. For Christmas every year, my grandmother would crochet or knit us new mittens, scarves, and hats. The brown, orange, and yellow zigzag-patterned afghan she made, and the patchwork one with the charcoal-colored squares of yarn flowers in pink, yellow, and purple, hung on our couch. One year, the mittens were in the pattern of animal heads.

Mittens were not easy for Bobby. He couldn't master the concept of putting his thumb in the thumbhole. He stood in front of my mother as she sat in a dining room chair. He held his hand out obediently. My mother put the mitten up to his hand. This one was the head of an elephant. The tongue was stitched on the inside of the hand. "Robert. Put. Your. Thumb. In. The. Hole."

She slid the mitten over his hand so the elephant ears were on top of his hand. His thumb ended up with the fingers, and the knitted thumb flapped lifelessly while the elephant's trunk hung from the top of his knuckles. He stared at her, quiet. He knew it was wrong. She took the mitten off, grabbed his hand, and pulled the thumb away from the fingers, his thumb now at a 90-degree angle. "Do it right this time, or you can't go outside," she said.

"Here. Let me try." I took the mitten from her and held Bobby's hand up. I didn't like it when she was frustrated or impatient with him and so I often tried to intervene. It would take about ten tries before the mittens were properly installed, and by the end of it,

Bobby would be crying and my mother would be worn out. Neither Bobby nor my mother understood what was wrong with their technique. I think my mother thought he did it on purpose to annoy her. I would be worn out too. Watching it made me nervous.

It would take me just as long to get his thumb in the thumbhole, but it was easier for me to do it myself than to see Bobby upset or my mother angry. I wanted my mother to be happy too and often felt like it was my responsibility to make sure she was. I worried that my mother resented Bobby. Maybe it was because he reminded her of her own brother or because she had to take him in. Perhaps I was just overly sensitive to it. I was always looking to protect Bobby from something. I never wanted him to feel alone, less than, or a nuisance. I wanted life to be easy for him. I wanted life to be easy for everybody I loved, but especially Bobby. I guess because his had started out so hard.

Eventually his thumb found its way into the right place and the mittens slid on. Once Bobby was properly bundled and every ounce of skin covered up except his nose for breathing and his eyes for seeing, he waddled outside to build snow forts with us or to ride the sled that my brother, Tim, pulled behind the snowmobile.

Bobby was addicted to his thumb. Even his mitten could not stop him from putting it in his mouth. Every pair had a hole at the thumb tip where he had sucked it through. Bobby continued this habit beyond the socially acceptable age of five or so. Trying to get him to give it up was another cause of frustration. My mother tried black pepper, crushed red pepper, and hot sauce, but he couldn't be stopped. She began to see that what had worked with her first four kids didn't always work with him.

Bobby loved his "nigh, nigh"—a pale yellow blanket with satin trim. It was the one thing he kept from those two paper bags my parents carried out along with him. He couldn't fall asleep without hugging this blanket, sucking his thumb, and rubbing the edge of the satin trim along his eyelid. My mother had to yank it out of his arms or steal it from his room in order to wash it. One summer day, she snuck it out of his bedroom for the laundry. Later that morning we found Bobby outside holding onto the blanket as it hung from the clothesline, thumb in his mouth, eyes closed. He had fallen asleep waiting for his blanket to dry.

We lived in a rural neighborhood that consisted of a string of houses on State Route 13. The houses were somewhat close together, with fifteen or so lined up on both sides of the street in a quarter mile stretch. Our place was at the top of the hill. It just so happened that most of the houses had children spread out over the same age group as us. We formed a band of kids. It seemed to be more boys than girls, which meant for a lot of years that my two sisters and I followed my older brother and his gang of friends all over the place. If they played PIG or HORSE on the Jones' basketball court, we stood on the sidelines and begged for a try. We insisted on playing football with them. The woods behind our house were a non-stop adventure as well, with vines to swing from and an over-sized boulder that Tim convinced me had an Indian chief buried under it and flecks of diamonds embedded in the rock that we could pound out with a smaller stone. There was also a pond. In the winter, my father would shovel off the snow so we could ice skate. Sometimes he would build a bonfire, and we'd roast hot dogs and marshmallows. We didn't carry bottled water with us then; it was unheard of. If we got thirsty, we would simply punch a hole in the ice and drink the pond water. In those days, we walked, ran, and biked all up and down this stretch of Route 13 with not much of a worry for pedophiles or kidnappers.

For some reason, there were no kids Bobby's age in our neighborhood. He was at least five years younger than the next oldest kid, which resulted in him playing by himself a lot of the time.

One afternoon when Bobby was four or five, he was playing alone in the sand pile. I would have been twelve, Patti was nine, Shelly was thirteen, and Tim, sixteen. Bobby sat on top of the six-foot-high mound and moved the dirt into a pile with the backhoe. He whistled as he used his loader to fill the box of the dump truck. Thanks to my dad's job at the gravel pit, we had the best sand pile in the neighborhood. He brought home a dump truck full of sand at the beginning of every summer.

Despite its height, my mother couldn't see the sand pile from the kitchen window; the shed was in the way. She checked the backyard every few minutes to make sure Bobby wasn't wandering around. She relied on our dog, Barfy, to help keep an eye on him. Barfy was always willing and patient while we rode around the yard on her back, patched with brown and black soft fur, holding her floppy ears like reins, ears that always heard the school bus and my dad's pick-up truck, her sloppy, wet face seeming to smile as she galloped to greet us.

Bobby pushed his yellow Tonka dump truck through the gravel pit he had built that summer, humming "puhpuhpuhpuh." His lips vibrated against themselves to make the motor sound. He drove it to the other side of the pit and dumped the load.

My mother noticed a strange car pull up out front. A man got out and walked into our yard. He moved quickly toward the shed, toward the sand pile. My mother ran outside. Before she could get to the man, 150 pounds of Saint Bernard charged straight at him. Barfy nailed his chest with her paws and knocked him to the ground. The man jumped up and ran away before my mother could get to him. Ronnie had been calling every few months, threatening to come and take Bobby, so my mother thought maybe she was behind it. Years later, Ronnie admitted to Bobby that she tried to kidnap him once.

I think this is another reason I felt so compelled to watch over and protect Bobby. His past was still an ominous presence in our lives that revealed itself every so often. I could sense the pull this darkness had on his life, even though he was safely rescued from all that and was growing up in the same house, the same way I grew up. I could sense that I had to remain vigilant to make sure he stayed in this place. He was part of my home now, and it was my job to keep everybody safe and happy in that home, or at least I acted like it was.

Most nights, we all flopped in the living room watching the only TV in our house. *Happy Days* was on, and we sat on the love seat and the couch sharing big bowls of popcorn. My dad sat in the big chair; that was his. As Potsie serenaded Joanie with the song, "Put Your Head on my Shoulder," Richie Cunningham played the drums, and Ralph Malph played the piano. Joanie sat on a stool, staring googly-eyed at Potsie while he sang.

Bobby stood in the middle of the living room floor, swaying and singing along.

"Put your hea on my yoldee," Bobby chimed in.

"Whisper in my ear, baby," I sang with him.

I scooped him up, held his left hand with my right, and we waltzed around the living room. He rested his head on my shoulder. "Tell me that you yuh me too."

Joanie was in love, and Bobby was asleep by the last line of the song. This became one of his favorite songs, and we would dance and sing it even without *Happy Days.*

On Christmas morning, we all woke up before my parents. We turned the television up and talked louder than normal to try and wake them. We knew our voices had a way of carrying down the hallway to the end where their room was. Our house was a one-story ranch. We moved in when I was two and stayed until after I graduated from college. There were five bedrooms off a long hallway with my parents at the end of a dogleg left. They had a sliding glass door that led out to the backyard, but the deck they had in mind was never built. We had one small bathroom, which wasn't so unheard of back then. Tim and Patti each had their own room, and Shelly and I shared a room. When Bobby was about two years old, he had moved out of the crib in my parents' room and into his own room. Bobby would leave his bed in the middle of the night, toddle down the hallway in his footed pajamas, and crawl in bed with one of us. Many mornings I woke up and found Bobby snuggling in bed with me. Some mornings we found him in the middle of our long hallway, sound asleep on the floor, rubbing the satin edge of his "nigh, nigh" on his cheek while he sucked his thumb. And some nights he slept by the wood stove in the living room. He hated to sleep alone.

Christmas presents were stacked under the tree from my parents and Santa. There was a cardboard fireplace against the wall—red brick with a cutout in the middle to hold the cardboard logs lit with flames—and extra logs for the fire and the andirons were painted on either side. My mother had hung our stockings from the mantle.

My parents finally woke up, and after they got their coffee, we sat around the living room in our pajamas, and my father handed out presents one at a time.

"To Kelly, from Bobby," my father announced as he picked up a present and walked toward me. The wrapping paper was lopsided and came just shy of covering the present completely, which Bobby tried to make up for with tape. The tape was clear, and I could see what it was before my father handed it to me.

"Make sure you guys are careful with the wrapping paper," my mother said. She folded the used wrapping paper and saved it for the next year.

I unwrapped the clay ashtray I had made in school; it had been on my dresser. "Wow. Thanks, Bobby. I love it." I said. He watched me from across the room with his shy, upside-down grin.

"To Mom, from Bobby." My father handed my mother a package. She unwrapped, very carefully, one of her favorite books off the shelf in the living room.

"Here's one for me, from Bobby." My father unwrapped one of the ties from his closet.

Every year, near Christmas and Bobby's birthday, letters or cards would arrive at our house with child-like scrawl on the envelope and pleadings on the outside:

Ma loves you, Robert.
I am his real mother.
Robert is my baby.

My mother didn't give the letters or cards to Bobby; she didn't want to upset him. She remembered what had happened when we first got him and Ronnie would visit. Bobby would shrink back into himself for a time. My mother didn't want to risk that happening again.

We never hid the adoption from Bobby, but we never really talked about it either. He was four years old when the adoption was finalized in court, and we were all there, including Bobby. There was no conspiracy to keep it a secret. There was no family meeting to make sure we were all on the same page. We didn't talk about it because we didn't need to. We went on with life as usual. Our family, friends, and neighbors knew—they remembered the day we got him and knew the story of how we fought to keep him. But nobody talked about it. He was just one of us, as if he had always been there, and to us, he had. We didn't tell him the dark details of his early life and the circumstances under which he was removed from his original home. We didn't tell him about George and Ronnie. We assumed he remembered more than he did.

Many years later, when I began the process of writing our story, Bobby and I had many conversations about what he remembered, and we had numerous sessions where I asked him specific questions to get his perspective on all of the moments captured in these pages. By the time we were both adults, we had been through so much together and had spent all of those years as soul mates, which allowed me access to Bobby's psyche like no one else in my life. I know his thoughts. I can read his feelings. I can talk to him on the phone and by the end of the first sentence know if he's in a good mood, tired, sick, or worried about something. I know when he won't look me in the eye that he has something bad to tell me, and I know when he fidgets with his hands and rocks back and forth in the chair that he's nervous, and I know when his brown eyes are open as far as they can go and he's not smiling that he's scared. I know his nervous laugh and the look he makes when he's about to cry. I'm not arrogant enough to think that I know every corner of his mind—or that I'm always 100 percent right—but I *know* him. I've made it my business to know him, to anticipate what he needs, how he's feeling, and what he would do in any situation. It was during one of these sessions that Bobby told me about the first time he knew there was something more to his story.

Bobby

I liked it inside my Transformers tent bed. It was kind of like camping only I got to stay in the house. This was my favorite present. I rubbed my full belly. Pork chops in cream of mushroom soup, mashed potatoes, and creamed corn. Yum. Mom always let me pick what I wanted for dinner on my birthday. Everybody around the table sang. Happy Birthday to you, Happy Birthday to you...Mom carried the cake out from its hiding place. Happy Birthday, dear Bobby...She set it down in front of me, and I blew out the eight candles. I opened my first card. "Read it," someone said. "Happy Birthday, Bobby," I'd read. A five-dollar bill dropped on the table. "From S...S...Stephen Huh...Hee..." I couldn't figure out how to say the last name. Everybody laughed. "Herbst. Stephen Herbst," someone yelled. "He's right there." My face turned hot and red. Stephen was nice and didn't say anything. I'd known Stephen my whole life. He was Timmy's best friend. He ate dinner with us all the time. I opened my next card but didn't read it out loud. Mom handed me her present. It was the tent bed. Exactly what I wanted.

It was quiet in the tent. I couldn't even hear the TV the other kids were watching in the living room. The walls of the tent hugged me. It was warm. The phone rang in the dining room. "Hello?" Mom said. "No. He's in bed." I was the only one in bed. It was too early for the others. "He doesn't need this right now. I'm not going to put him on the phone," Mom said. Who was she talking to? I had a feeling it was about me. Who would call me on my birthday? At nighttime? Nobody ever called me. And why wouldn't Mom let me talk? I'd heard other things, things that made me wonder. And I knew there were strange letters and cards that came in the mail sometimes; they said Robert Boulay on them. I didn't know who that was. Mom always took the letters. Not sure what she did with them.

I zipped my tent and closed my eyes. I was tired. Sad my birthday was over. I didn't tell anyone what I'd heard that night or ask Mom who was on the phone. I was pretty sure it was about me. But I kept it to myself and wondered.

...one of those women

WHAT DO YOU THINK WOULD BE MOST EFFECTIVE to work on today?" Dr. Marsha asked. Her pen was poised over a yellow pad ready to take notes. As usual, I didn't know how to answer that question. I began to tell her about a recent revelation I'd had about Kevin and his self-destructive behavior. After hours spent analyzing and thinking about it, I believed I wasn't the intended target for his hurt, I was just "collateral damage." After I finished, I waited for Dr. Marsha to exclaim how impressed she was with my insight.

"Maybe you're right. I'll work with Kevin on that. But this is *your* time, I'd rather talk about you, Kelly," she said.

"Oh."

That was always more difficult for me. I was an expert on why other people did the things they did, why they hurt, what their feelings were. It was much harder for me to understand my own feelings. Dr. Marsha wouldn't let me get away that easily. She pushed me.

"So tell me how you're feeling," she said.

"I don't know. I just keep thinking about how for my entire life

I've never wanted to be one of *those women*," I said, using my first two fingers on each hand as air quotes.

"What women?" Dr. Marsha countered.

"You know. The poor, powerless, pathetic wife, trapped at home, while her husband is out doing whatever he wants to do."

"You mean like your mother?" Dr. Marsha asked.

I knew the first thirteen years of my parents' marriage were ugly. In those years, my mother was depressed and unhappy. Even though I was very young, on some level I knew this and believed that if I was a good girl, made sure everybody was happy and okay, then my dad wouldn't leave us and my mother would smile and laugh. I desperately wanted to make my mother happy. Maybe because my earliest family story about myself is that my mother cried when she found out she was pregnant with me. I had known this story as long as I could remember, and it didn't bother me. I understood her. I understood that she had two kids already, my sister, Shelly, only three months old, and she felt trapped in a world that offered her nothing. Was this why I'd spent the rest of my life trying to make my mother happy?

She hadn't had an easy life, even before she married my father. Her parents were divorced, her mother an alcoholic. She thought she'd earned a way out of that life when good grades landed her a college scholarship, but for a reason I still don't understand, her mother wouldn't let her go. I knew from the age of sixteen that she'd had to take care of herself, working just to make sure she had food to eat and a roof overhead.

My mother used to say, "If I had to do it all over again, I wouldn't have kids." I don't remember how old I was the first time I heard it, and she doesn't remember saying it. But she did, and it was okay. It was said without malice; I knew my mother loved me. And I knew she wanted to leave. I knew that night at the front door, where my sister and I stood with the icy air blowing up our flannel night-gowns, screaming, crying, begging her not to leave. She didn't. I knew she had nowhere to go and no money to get there.

My mother began telling me as I got older to make sure I "married rich." I would defiantly respond with "I'll make my own money." I never dreamt of my wedding, like many girls do. I never thought about the dress I would wear or if I'd get married on a beach or in a church. I never dreamt of how many babies I would have and what their names would be.

Dr. Marsha explained to me that day in her office that all of these things I'd witnessed at such a young age with my mother were the reason I had the career that I had, the reason I was diligent about financial security, the reason I didn't have children. I would never be my mother. I would never be dependent on a man. I would never be trapped with five kids and no money. I thought this would also protect me from my husband cheating on me. Apparently, I made all of these subconscious decisions so young that I never remembered making them at all, but I had known it my whole life.

It would be easy to resent my mother for all these things, but it actually made me love her more. She did have a choice; she could have left us all. She could have run away and never looked back. She could have turned to alcohol or drugs herself or looked for solace with another man or her girlfriends, but she didn't. She stayed. She worked. She fought for her family. It took tremendous strength for her to stay, to raise us kids despite what was going on around her. My mother didn't lie in bed all day, covers pulled up over her head and crying. She got up every morning, toast and cereal waiting for us, the radio in the kitchen playing the news at low volume while we got ready for school. My mother met us when we got off the bus and cooked dinner every night. I watched her take care of the alcoholic mother who hadn't taken care of her. We saw my grandmother at least once a week when my mother visited her trailer to make sure she was eating. I remember many times we found her at her favorite bar, The Verona Beach Hotel, instead of her trailer.

I was never quite comfortable walking into a bar in the middle of the day but went anyway so my mother didn't have to go alone. The regulars would be there with their gin grins and watery eyes, pretending as if there was no place else they should be. When our eyes recovered from the temporary blindness caused by bright sunlight colliding with smoky bar light, we'd see my grandmother on her favorite stool with her glass of Genny draft in front of her. The high-backed stool seemed to swallow her in her navy tracksuit with her size four feet in matching Keds hanging six inches from the floor.

My mother didn't have much of a support network and couldn't find anyone else to watch us when her friend won a free trip for four to Puerto Rico. So they left us with my grandmother for a week, I'm sure with fingers crossed that she'd stay out of the bars and keep sober. I don't remember much excitement that week except that I developed a skin rash, and my forearms became blotchy red and itchy. My grandmother called the doctor's office and made an appointment for me in the middle of a school day to make sure my scarlet fever hadn't returned. When she walked into my third-grade classroom, straight to the teacher's desk with her attachable sunglasses flipped up on her frames, talking too loudly, my face burned, and I wanted to crawl under my desk. My parents brought us wooden maracas and straw sombreros with *Puerto Rico* stitched in red letters across the top.

Even though I didn't have any happy memories of my grandmother, I didn't resent her either. I still wonder what happened to her when she was a girl that compelled her to live the way she did.

Rather than a victim, I began to see my mother, with her barely five-foot petite frame, as a warrior—a quiet, often misunderstood, often unappreciated warrior. One who would stand by her husband, with her children, and would fight for her nephew, Bobby, when he needed to be rescued.

After that session with Dr. Marsha, I went home and lay down on my bed. I was suddenly more tired than I'd ever been. I cried. I cried all through dinner, through the rest of that night, and the next day. I had always been so secure in my non-motherhood, so convinced that I didn't want children and never had, that I married someone who didn't want more than the two he already had, then convinced him to have a vasectomy. The more I thought about these things, I knew Dr. Marsha was right on. I didn't want to believe I had never truly understood myself all these years. The most painful realization was that I knew my time had passed. There will be no one on this earth who has my eyes, or my laugh, or my voice. There's no better version of me on the way. But what really gnawed at me was this question: If I had discovered these things about myself ten years ago, would I have made different choices? *Could I have been a mother?*

GONE

BOBBY STARTED TO LIE AROUND THE SAME TIME puberty settled in. He would lie about almost anything and everything. He lied about brushing his teeth, cleaning his room, or leaving the television on all night. Bobby was eleven years old, and the easygoing little boy had become much more difficult to live with. I left for college around that same time. My older sister, Shelly, was away at college as well. Tim had already finished his bachelor's degree and was working and living on his own. I didn't think I had to worry about things at home. I thought Bobby was fine. I was wrong. He and my mother fought on a daily basis and were always at war over something—going to school, doing homework, lies he had told. "Mom always found something I did wrong," he once told me.

By the time I came home from college, he was stealing. My mother had a garage sale and earned a few hundred dollars. Bobby took that money. He took money from her purse. He lied to cover his tracks but almost always got caught. The key was not asking him if he took the garage sale money but instead asking him why he stole the money from the garage sale. Starting with the assumption that you already knew tripped him up. He would stumble over his words without looking you in the eye and eventually say something to incriminate himself.

I met Kevin in my last year of college. He was eight years older than I was, with an ex-wife and two sons, the oldest was eleven, the youngest one, seven. Instead of taking my twenties to enjoy my freedom and independence, I settled down immediately, and we bought a house just a mile up the road from my parents. I renewed my focus on making sure my family was happy, safe, and at peace, adding it to my list of adult responsibilities—budding accounting career, home of my own, and live-in boyfriend with kids. Bobby was the last one left at home now. Patti was twenty, happily married, staying at home full-time with her two babies, and living next door to my parents. Shelly was twenty-four and working in a law firm, also married, with a baby girl; she too lived close by. Tim had his own place and was enjoying life in his twenties as a bachelor. I tried to relieve the tension between Bobby and my mother by getting him out of the house. He would come and stay with me on the weekends when Kevin's two young sons visited. Bobby became close friends with them.

He also showed up at my house or one of my sisters' houses when we weren't home and would take things—clothes, gasoline out of the can in the garage, change left on the dresser, anything of value that was accessible. We had to lock our doors.

He started hanging out with a new kid up the street who introduced him to cigarettes, pot, and porn. Bobby used his stolen funds to pay for his new bad habits. Bobby's bedroom was on the second floor and had a fire escape ladder in it. He used it to sneak out in the middle of the night. One night, they took his friend's mother's car for a joy ride. He also did silly things that irked my mother—he left the freezer unplugged in the garage and hundreds of dollars of food was lost. If he didn't feel like going downstairs to the one bathroom in the house, he peed out the second story window.

Even with all Bobby was doing to hurt and frustrate the people around him, I found a way to defend him. He was acting out for a reason. He was misunderstood. I intervened between him and my mother. I negotiated arguments between him and my brother and sisters when he stole from them. I tried to keep the peace. Bobby's school life was just as frustrating as his home life. It seemed the older he got, the more difficult it became for him. I knew he was struggling but at the time didn't realize how much or why. With all the trouble he'd been in lately, I assumed he didn't do his homework and cut classes just to piss off my mother. It would be almost fifteen years before I discovered the real reason.

I rallied everyone to support him whenever I could. On a sunny day at the end of May, I lined up as many as I could to watch the Memorial Day parade in town. Bobby was in ninth grade at Canastota Junior/Senior High and had recently joined the marching band in an attempt to belong and be normal. This was his debut performance.

My sisters and I found the best corner to place our lawn chairs. My sisters' kids laughed at the clowns and ran into the street to pick up the candy they tossed. My parents and Kevin were there. After the little league, the fire department, the veterans, and the American Legion Auxiliary marched by, we heard music in the distance. "Here he comes," I shouted. We heard the trumpets, the clarinets and flutes, the drums, all coming closer to us. We searched the formation for Bobby. We stepped up on our tiptoes to see over the bouncing heads of the band. "Bobbee-Bobbee-Bobbee," we chanted, unable to see him yet but hoping he could hear us over the music. Rows of uniformed band members marched by. Then we saw him, marching in the last row, a bass drum strapped to his chest. "Way to go, Bobbeeee," we yelled, cheering and clapping, making a scene in the subdued crowd as he banged out the baseline to "The Right Stuff" by New Kids On The Block. He stared straight ahead, focused on his drum beat.

But as much as I tried to support Bobby, having him at my house so I could keep him out of trouble, no matter how much I defended him and made excuses for him, he seemed intent on rebelling. My grandfather had given my mother his treasured collection of twenty-five silver dollars before he died. My mother thought the coins were well hidden until one day she noticed they were missing.

"Why did you take my silver coins, Robert?" she asked.

"I don't know. I didn't take 'em," he replied. Bobby wouldn't meet her eyes and nervously shifted from one foot to the other.

"That was the very last thing my father ever gave me. Why would you do that to me?"

Bobby said nothing and walked away from her.

"I can't have anything around here," my mother said. She began locking the office door after that.

My parents attended a small church, and my mother helped the pastor with the weekly collection. She carried the money home in an envelope on Sunday afternoon. She counted the money in her office, prepared the bank deposit, and paid the electric and fuel oil bill for the church. She always left the money organized in order of denomination and filed the checks alphabetically. She started to notice that her envelope was disorganized, bills out of place, not how she left it. She had a gut feeling she knew what was happening and started to notice she couldn't account for all the money that should have been there. One day she saw Bobby coming out of the office. "Why are you stealing money from the collection?" my mother asked. Bobby avoided her eyes and shrugged his shoulders.

"It's not even my money. Why would you steal from church?" Bobby didn't have an answer for her. My mother stopped bringing the money home after that. Keeping the door locked wasn't enough to stop him from stealing.

I spent a lot of time trying to figure out why Bobby was acting the way he was. I was so sure that if I could figure out the reason, I could fix it. When Bobby turned sixteen, I thought it might help him to know more about his biological parents. He had figured out that he was adopted, but that was all he knew. I thought his curiosity could be the reason he was acting out. Maybe he resented my parents for not telling him earlier. Maybe he resented them because he was adopted. I convinced my parents it was a good idea to tell him everything, so they did. They told him about George and Ronnie and the adoption but left out the darkest details of the abuse and neglect that surrounded his first ten months of life. Bobby didn't have much of an emotional response when they talked to him, at least not on the surface, which was typical for him. Oftentimes, it was hard to gauge what Bobby was feeling based on his reaction to things. My parents gave Bobby the last address and phone number they had for George and Ronnie.

My family was about to enter a period of unraveling. Not only for Bobby, but for my entire family, for me. At the same time this was happening with Bobby and my parents, my younger sister had decided she didn't want to be married anymore and left her husband and her two babies. She had married her high school sweetheart, and he had been like a son to my parents and a brother to me. My older sister left her husband about four months later. I mourned for their broken homes. I cried tears that weren't mine to cry. I sobbed over my nieces' and nephew's heartbreak as if it were my own heartbreak, as if they were my own children caught in the middle, as if it were my own home breaking up. I felt like it was.

One night my parents came back from dinner, and my sister, who lived next door, had a U-Haul truck in the driveway to pack up her belongings. I stood in the driveway with Kevin as my parents got out of the car. They quickly realized what was happening and why the U-Haul was there.

"I'm so fuckin' sick of this," my mother said to no one in particular. She walked into the house. I had never heard my mother curse like that before, and I haven't since. I felt like I was losing control. My family was falling apart and I didn't know how to stop it. My four-year-old nephew cried at the front door after his mom left, his body convulsing with sobs in my arms, his face and T-shirt soaked with tears, snot, and saliva. He got so upset he threw up on me, his vomit filling the pocket of my sweatshirt. The screaming, the crying, the sadness, the brokenness, unraveled me. I remembered what it felt like to beg my mom not to leave, standing at our front door in my nightie. What was happening to my nephew had been my own worst fear.

My parents had an unnerving and annoying habit of surrendering everything to God. They prayed endlessly and loved unconditionally. Their faith sustained them. It pissed me off. I wanted action. I wanted them to do something. I wanted them to fight for our family. I know now that they were fighting, just in a different way than I was. I professed faith as well and I prayed. I cried out to God when I woke up in the morning, in my car at lunchtime, and in my bed at night. I just didn't trust him to answer. I ate ice cream. I drank beer. I lost sleep. I lost tears. I lost hope. I lost my home.

These people were my home. Although we no longer lived together under one roof, they were my home. They were the walls I needed around me to feel safe. To feel loved. The warm blanket covering me in my bed at night, with the house still, no one screaming, no one threatening to leave, no one drunk, safely tucked in with peace and quiet. I needed them to stay in place. The twenty-something woman I was at that time was still convinced she had to keep them together, keep the peace, keep her home, keep Bobby.

Telling Bobby the truth about his adoption and biological parents seemed to backfire, at least to me. It didn't stop him from fighting with my mother. It didn't stop his lying or stealing. My mother found pornographic magazines in his bedroom, in the barn, and in the piano bench. When she confronted him he became angry and belligerent. "Robert, I will not tolerate that in my house," she told him.

"If I can't do what I want, I'm leaving," Bobby said. "I don't have to take this."

My father tried to intervene. Sitting on the edge of his bed that night, he asked Bobby to try harder—with his mother, with school, with the lying and stealing. He thought he got through to him. But later, in the middle of the night, Bobby packed his duffel bag and left. He walked to a friend's house and stayed there for a couple of weeks. My parents had no idea where he was.

I also believed that the strife happening with my sisters and their families, and my parents, upset Bobby. He had always hated arguing and conflict and was sad to lose both of his brothers-in-law in a short period of time.

"Kelly, there's nothing we can do. If he wants to go, we can't force him to stay," my mother said. We had been arguing on the phone.

We argued a lot about Bobby. He had contacted George and Ronnie and asked if he could come live with them. He made arrangements to meet them in Cortland, New York, halfway between Binghamton and our home. Bobby called and asked my parents for a ride. My mother and father were planning to drive him to Cortland the next day to meet George and Ronnie.

"You can try harder to stop him. He's only sixteen!" I said. "You don't have to drive him." I was furious with my parents for letting him go. They didn't try hard enough. I was sick at the thought of him spending any time with the two people who had done those horrible things to him as a baby. It was my fault. It was my idea to tell him about his biological parents. I was wrong. We failed him. I failed him. This wasn't part of the plan. It wasn't part of my plan. I didn't want to let him go without a fight.

"You can beg him. Tell him how much you don't want him to go. Tell him they're evil and he'll waste years of his life with them."

"Your father tried talking to him. He won't listen to us," my mother insisted.

I second-guessed the approach they were taking, but I wasn't living in the house with them. I didn't think it would work for him to move in with me. My house was a small two-bedroom, and I didn't think it was right to move Bobby into the room that belonged to Kevin's sons when they visited us on the weekends. I'm sure my parents were exhausted from fighting with Bobby to get him to realize the consequences of his actions. Those dark, ominous forces from his past seemed to be pulling him in a direction that none of us could stop. We had kept him this long. It destroyed me to think that all of that was coming undone.

My parents didn't think they had a choice, so they gave Bobby the choice—come back home or go live with George and Ronnie. He chose George and Ronnie. Bobby's last day of ninth grade was on a Friday. He dropped out of the school that had quit on him long ago. He left home the next day.

Saturday morning, my parents drove Bobby to Cortland. They pulled into a McDonald's parking lot. George and Ronnie were already there. My father parked a few spaces away. Bobby got out and grabbed his duffel bag from the back seat. My mother stayed in the car, fighting her tears, trying hard not to cry. My father got out and walked with him. "Make sure he goes to school," he told George and Ronnie. He hugged Bobby and walked back to his car.

My parents were quiet as they rode home that day. They thought of the trip they took on that same road, fifteen years ago, with Bobby on the floor of the van between them. They remembered how he looked up at them with his brown eyes that reflected their own relief, thinking they had saved him. They remembered how easy he was as a little boy, easier than the other kids in a lot of ways. *Where had they gone wrong?*

And as suddenly as he came into our home, he was gone.

PART TWO

LOST

RUNAWAY TRAIN

RUNAWAY TRAIN NEVER GOING BACK, WRONG WAY on a one way track…" I had to stop and catch my breath before I could sing the next line. Kevin was driving us home from Binghamton while I sobbed and sang this 1993 Soul Asylum song, over and over and over again.

I hadn't been able to find Bobby on this trip. Kevin had been a good sport as I told him to turn left and then right and was patient when I looped the same few blocks for a couple of hours. I looked and looked and looked in all the places I thought he might be. I checked all the streets Bobby had mentioned on the collect phone calls we'd had every so often since he'd run away at sixteen to live with George and Ronnie. He was eighteen now and had been gone for two years. It seemed like forever.

I felt like Bobby was right there that day, within reach. He was close, I knew it. I kept expecting him to walk around the corner onto Munsell Street any minute. And I was convinced he probably showed up as soon as we turned our car north and headed home. Who knows? He could have been in that three-story dark green house with the Doberman Pinschers on the roof. He could have told that skinny rat-man to lie and say he hadn't seen him in weeks. He could have been watching me from some window in some other house in the neighborhood, waiting for me to give up on him.

"Bought a ticket for a runaway train, like a madman laughin' at the rain, little out of touch, little insane, just easier than dealing with the pain..." My voice was shaky but I sang anyway. I blew my nose and pulled my map out again. I stared at the streets in the neighborhood I knew he was in. I ran my fingers along the crease and over the pen marks I had made on the map. I looked for a street I had missed.

The worst part for me when Bobby ran away to live with George and Ronnie was that I never really knew where he was. He didn't last very long living with them, and they had even moved to Pennsylvania recently without him. So much for them wanting their son back. After that, Bobby roamed aimlessly around Binghamton. I never had a phone number where I could reach him. At night, when I closed my eyes on another day without him home, I would see his face, his eyes. Until that moment when sleep would rescue my mind, I imagined my teenaged brother wandering the streets without enough clothes to keep him warm or a place to lay his head. I imagined him hungry. I imagined people hurting him. I knew he would talk to strangers, he would offer help to anyone who needed it and give what little money he had in his pocket to whoever asked for it. I also knew that the unfamiliar streets and people would take advantage of him, steal his money, that he would trust people he shouldn't. I knew he would be scared. I remembered that when he was a little boy he hated to sleep alone.

I also knew I wouldn't stop looking for him. I would keep driving to Binghamton. I would drive down every street and knock on as many doors as I needed to. I wouldn't give up until I found Bobby and convinced him to come back home.

Bobby

I went over the floor again with the mop. I was just moving the dirt around. No matter what I tried I couldn't get rid of the scum. I wiped down the counter in the kitchen, cleaned the couch in the living room. Didn't seem to make much of a difference. Didn't know how I could get the yellow off the walls. Ronnie's place was even dirtier because of her dogs. I didn't understand why George and Ronnie didn't live together since they were still married. I was staying with George on Robinson Street. Ronnie lived on Lyon Street with her boyfriend, but she was over here all the time. She was weird. The first night I was here she wanted to sleep in the same bed as me. No way that was gonna happen.

In the first week I was there, George and Ronnie took me to Social Services and signed me up as their dependent so they could get extra food stamps and money. They took me everywhere they went. Told everybody I was their son. That was weird. It was embarrassing, with their dirty clothes and greasy hair. The kids in the neighborhood called her "Plunger" 'cause she never wore her teeth and her face sunk in.

Everybody said how much I looked like my father. I felt sorry for him. I could see he was afraid to stand up to Ronnie. I'd seen Ronnie throw glasses at the wall, punch things if she didn't get her way. At the beginning of the month, when she had money, she would drink a lot. My father drank three beers every night. That didn't seem so bad.

I could tell they were getting sick of me too. They complained that I ate too much and took too many showers. At least I showered. More than I could say for them. So much for living with my "real" parents.

*I thought it would be better than that. I thought it would be differ-
ent. I thought they would be happy to have me back, that I would
fit in better with them than I did at home. But that didn't happen.
Same disappointment there. Everywhere I went I felt like I wasn't
enough. George and Ronnie just told me they were moving with two
other men to Reading, Pennsylvania. They didn't ask me to move with
them. I didn't want to go anyway. I knew the parents I had dreamt
about didn't exist, and the reality of my roots hit me hard. I thought
about going home but didn't think Mom wanted me either. I wished I
could get my own place. My own home. Maybe someday.*

*As I moved the mop around the kitchen floor one more time, I
thought about the house I would get someday, with my own garage
for my tools and a yard. I would keep it cleaner than this. That's for
sure. And no dogs.*

After George and Ronnie left him for Pennsylvania, Bobby wandered from house to house, staying on friends' couches, eating
meals at the soup kitchen, trying to figure out what to do next.

It would be some years later, when I served meals at our local
Rescue Mission every other Sunday, that I would wonder who
among us was more beyond hope than someone without a place to
lay their head at night? A place that is dry of rain and snow, shielded
from wind and cold, a place to call home? When I handed men with
empty eyes their plate of macaroni and cheese or bologna sandwich, men who had coldness settled in their bones, I thought of my
brother eating alone in a soup kitchen. When I looked at the man I
was serving, I thought about the sister or mother he had somewhere,
and I knew she was lying awake at night, wondering where he was

and if he was okay, praying that someone would take care of him. I wanted to call her and tell her that he was okay. He ate tonight. He's safe. I wanted to tell her what I wanted to hear, what I needed to know.

I begged Bobby to come home every chance I had. I offered him my couch to sleep on. I tried to find just the right words to convince him that he belonged here, with us. Once or twice it seemed to work, and he would show up on my doorstep. He would stay just long enough for my hopes to rise, but when I woke up the next day he would be gone without a word. He seemed to have some sort of instinct, something in him that called him back to George and Ronnie and the town he was born in. Like a homing pigeon that flies back to the same place, no matter the distance he had travelled in the opposite direction, no matter the forces trying to keep him where he was.

On one of his surprise visits home, Bobby brought his new girl-friend, and they decided to stay a while. They slept on my couch for a few weeks. This was the first time Bobby had been home for more than a day or two in a couple of years. He asked me to help him find a place to live. Kevin and I set them up in an apartment close by and we got them some used furniture. I would do anything to keep him, anything to get my peace back, anything to appease my guilt. I believed then that if I had been a better sister, spent more time with him when he was younger, he wouldn't have left. If I had helped him with his schoolwork, his grades would have been better, maybe he would have stayed. Mostly, I just felt helpless.

But this time I was hopeful. His apartment wasn't far from my house, and he had already talked to a few people about a job. It seemed like he was home for good.

A few days passed without a phone call from Bobby. A week went by and I didn't see him. A familiar dread grew in my stomach. I got in my car and drove to his apartment.

I knocked on his door. No answer. "Bobby? Are you there?" I yelled. "Bobby?" I didn't want to use my key unless I was sure no one was home.

"Bob. Open up. It's me." I knocked again, a little harder.

"Bobbee." I heard nothing. I used my key to open the door.

I felt the emptiness as soon as I stepped in. He was gone.

Bobby

I pulled my hat tighter, trying to keep the snow from trickling down my neck. I wished I had a warmer coat and a pair of boots. It had only been a few minutes since my dad and Ronnie dropped me off on Route 81 and already my toes were cold. I knew it was about a two-hour drive to Binghamton and wondered how long it would take to walk if no one picked me up.

I started to wonder if I did the right thing, taking off again, but I just couldn't stand Ronnie. I'd been calling George Dad, but I just couldn't call her Mom. Never would. And I would rather take my chances out here, freeze to death, or get kidnapped by a serial killer than put up with her anymore. It had been a couple of months since I left that apartment Kelly got me in Canastota. I felt bad leaving without telling her, but I was so mad when my girlfriend left me to go back to Binghamton. I called Dad and Ronnie. They drove up from Pennsylvania that night and took me back to Shenandoah. They had rented half a house there. I slept in the living room on the couch. There were two other men living with them. Franklin had his own room, and my father had his own room. Ronnie and her boyfriend, Anthony, lived in the attic. Franklin and Anthony both lived on Social

Security; Ronnie handled their money. George got disability and SSI, but he wouldn't let Ronnie touch his money. He didn't trust her. She spent money on herself and things she didn't need. She bought a refrigerator that she kept in her room. She put food in it that she didn't want anyone else to have. Nobody was allowed in her room, especially me. She let Anthony have whatever he wanted, but not Franklin. Sometimes Franklin wanted things like pipe tobacco, and Ronnie told him no, he didn't need it. I felt bad leaving Franklin behind with her. Ronnie had three dogs, a rabbit, and a bird. The animals ate better than they did. Franklin got to the point where he would not come out of his room to eat because the house stank of animals, and Ronnie would not let him eat in his room because he always made a mess.

I thought it would be better when they moved from that place to the old apartment building in Girardville. At least I would have my own room. Except no one was allowed in the bathroom because the dogs were locked in there all the time. They shit all over the floor and the tub. I couldn't take a shower or use the toilet. Ronnie had two toilet chairs, like the ones old people use. She made us use those stupid chairs whenever we needed to go to the bathroom. That's what really pushed me over the edge. That and her stupid refrigerator with the lock on it. Only she and Anthony had the key. Why should I have to beg for food? She never let me have any of the soda in there. Ronnie found two more men to move in, and that's when I knew I had to get out.

I jumped every time a car whizzed by, and the icy slush splashed on me, soaking my pants and sneakers. I wished it would stop snowing. I was afraid to stick my thumb out, thought it was against the law to hitchhike. Maybe that guy, Frank, would let me sleep on his couch again. I knew somebody would let me crash. I would have to find a ride back down here to get my stuff. I didn't take the time to pack, and I really couldn't carry it anyway. It was just starting to get dark when a truck pulled up behind me and offered me a ride.

A TICKET FOR HOME

I WALKED DOWN THE AISLE ON MAY 27, 1995, ON THE ARM of my almost seven-year-old nephew. He was in his shiny suit and tie, his small, bony arm at a ninety-degree angle, his face serious and determined. My father waited at the altar for me; he had been ordained at the age of fifty-five and began a new career as a minister. He married us that day, his first of many weddings. In my custom-made but plain white dress, I carried lilies. I hooked onto my nephew's arm and walked toward my father and Kevin, resisting the urge to look behind me to see if Bobby was there.

I had told Bobby I was getting married. I told him the date and time and where it would take place. "Please come home for it," I said to him. "I'll come get you."

"I'll send you bus money."

"I really want you there."

He never said if he would or wouldn't come. His silence was like a seed of hope that took root inside me, even though I knew it was risky and could end up being crushed. I carried this hope with me while I planned my wedding day. Whenever anyone asked me about my wedding, I felt that seed growing, just a little. Hoping he would come, that he would want to be there as much as I wanted him.

The past few years of unraveling had left me sad and depressed most days. I didn't spend much time thinking about myself, my career, my hopes and dreams, or getting married. I was waiting for Bobby to come home, for my sisters to come to their senses, waiting for everyone else to behave like I needed them to. I was waiting for my home to be put back in order first, then I could relax and think about me.

But in an uncharacteristic moment of thinking about my life, I decided, *Screw it. I'm getting married.* I was going to forget about the fact that my little brother was gone and my sisters were divorcing and my nieces and nephews were getting yanked all over the place. I made a decision to do something for me. *Good for you. Focus on your own life, Kelly.* I was my own hero—for a day or two anyway. That cavalier, self-indulgent moment was fleeting. I kept up a good front, but in my heart and mind I wanted Bobby to be there. I didn't want to get married without him.

In the days and weeks leading up to the wedding, I was disappointed when I came home from work and Bobby wasn't waiting on my doorstep. He would do that sometimes, just show up. Or call me out of the blue from the bus stop and say, "Hey, I need a ride." But that didn't happen.

Still, after Kevin and I said our vows and kissed, I expected to turn toward the guests and see him in the back row. He'd have snuck in during the ceremony, stolen a seat in the back, getting there just in time to surprise me. That didn't happen.

I danced with my husband to "Let me call you sweetheart, I'm in love with you..." I danced with my father. I smiled. I watched the pianist play his music. I looked over my shoulder, looking for Bobby. I danced with my four-year-old nieces dressed in their blue-striped, flouncy dresses, which twirled when they did. I looked at the door. I was annoyed that no one else seemed to be missing him. I wasn't like this just because it was my wedding. I felt this way on every Christmas, Thanksgiving, Easter, birthday, or Sunday dinner—my whole family around the table, enjoying food and each other's company, together again, yet not complete.

The guests sat around white-covered round tables with lilies in the center. The Caesar salad, stuffed chicken breast, and twice-baked potatoes were served. The small room in the antique church was lit by candles, which cast a warm glow on all of us. But I was haunted by Bobby's empty chair.

After the three-tiered strawberry cheesecake had been cut, and someone had snapped the picture of Kevin and I feeding it to each other, my hope was trampled, a disappointment I couldn't let go of long enough to enjoy a day I'll never have again.

Bobby

I stood in the middle as five or six guys stood around me in a circle. The first punch landed hard on my jaw. Actually hurt worse than I thought it would. Since they let the smaller guys in the gang do the initiation, I thought it would hurt less. The second punch hit me hard in the back, didn't see that one coming. One kicked me in the groin. It was hard not to fall to my knees. I just had to keep standing.

The Puerto Rican Posse lived upstairs from my efficiency apartment on the ground floor. They started hanging out on my porch not long after I moved in, smoking pot all day. They said I earned the right to join the gang after what happened at Kmart.

I'd been in Kmart with one of the PRP. We walked through the store. My friend picked up a car stereo off the shelf and put it under his coat. I acted cool. I knew enough not to say anything. We walked down that store aisle and kept right on walking, right out the front door. Seemed pretty easy.

"Hey Robert, carry the stereo for me?" my friend asked when we were walking home. I shrugged and took it from him. A few minutes later, a pickup truck with two guys in it drove up behind us, rolled down their window, and asked for directions. I stopped, thought I'd try to help them find whatever they were looking for. My friend took off. The guys in the truck flashed their IDs; they were security guards from Kmart. I was caught. They looked at the stereo in my arms. I looked around, figured my friend was home by now. I couldn't think of anything to say. The guards wrote me an appearance ticket and charged me with petit larceny. I never snitched on my new friends, so they said I could join the gang if I had the guts to go through the initiation.

With each punch the pain was a little easier. I was a little more numb. The joint they'd given me before they started the beating also helped. The fists, knees, and feet seemed to pound me for an hour when someone finally yelled, "Times up." I was still standing. The same guys who had just punched me, kicked me, and pushed me for twenty minutes without stopping, now high-fived me, slapped my back—bruised purple from top to bottom—and shook my hand. I was one of them now.

Saturday morning must be a slow time for bailing people out of jail. The waiting room was empty. I was the only one. The chairs and the floor were the same shade of dishwater gray as the dingy walls. There were no windows. I couldn't imagine what it was like on the other side of that steel door. I stared at the round, white clock on the wall, the second hand clicking as it moved through hours of waiting. Bobby had called me earlier that week to tell me he'd been arrested for missing a court appearance and asked for three hundred dollars in bail money.

"There's nothing for you there. Come home. You can get a job here, get your GED," I pleaded.

"Mom doesn't want me to come home."

"Yes, she does, and who cares anyway? You can stay at my house as long as you need to."

When he told me about his gang initiation it felt like a fist wrapped around my heart and squeezed until it physically hurt. I couldn't understand why he stood there and let those guys beat him until he bruised. I couldn't understand why he would put himself through that. He was rescued from violence. Why would he go back to it? I had driven to Binghamton to see for myself if he was okay. My younger sister was dating a guy at the time who was six foot two and 240 pounds, so I recruited them to come with me and Kevin. We found the apartment building where Bobby and the gang lived, and somehow I convinced Kevin and my sister's boyfriend to go in the building and look around for Bobby. A couple of guys followed them up the stairs.

"Who you looking for?" they asked.

"Bobby. Robert. You seen him?" The two guys seemed to relax a little when they said they were looking for Bobby.

"He's not here. You got any smokes?" We didn't find Bobby that day.

The landlord liked Bobby because he helped him paint and clean empty apartments, getting them ready for new tenants. He convinced Bobby to move to another of his apartment buildings because he wanted to help him get away from the gang. The landlord was getting ready to evict them. It wasn't long after Bobby moved out that the cops busted in one afternoon and arrested most of the PRP for drugs.

Jail was good leverage and I was confident this time. I told Bobby I would bail him out if he would come home with me and stay at my house while he got a job and his GED. No one else would bail him out. He promised me he was ready this time.

The silence made me jumpy. The solid metal door buzzed; Bobby walked in the room.

"Hi." He looked down, avoiding my eyes.

"Hi. Are you okay?" I asked.

I noticed a new mark on his lower right arm—a cross with "Love" written on it and a flower and ribbon wrapped around it. "Did you get that in jail?" I asked.

"No, a friend of mine did it. He has his own tattoo gun." This was the latest in his growing ink collection: on his right shoulder he had a double heart with a unicorn, his lower left arm had a smiley face with a knife through it, and on his right bicep was the name "Heather" flanked by two flowers. His tattoos were all faded even though they were new. Every time I saw him, I noticed more of a change in him, his eyes a little emptier and veiled in sadness.

His hair was long and dirty. I remembered the soft blond hair that crowned his head as a little boy. It had grown darker with each passing year, as blond hair sometimes does, until it was dark brown. Now it was long and greasy.

I shaved his hair with clippers for him every time he came home. The first time I shaved it for him we were in my parents' garage.

Bobby sat in a folding chair, and I stood behind him with the clippers.

"What are these numbers on the side?" I whispered to Kevin. I was trying to pretend I knew what I was doing, but the truth was I had never cut anyone's hair with clippers before.

"I thought you knew what you were doing." Bobby shifted in the chair.

"Don't worry, it's fine," I said.

Kevin leaned over and moved the setting to number three and gave me the thumbs up.

"Okay, here goes nothing," I said.

I took the clippers and swiped the long hairs below his neck first, watching the greasy curls fall to the cement floor.

"This is fun!" I said.

Bobby and Kevin exchanged glances.

Once the longest part was gone, I started above his forehead and tried to make even strokes from the front to the crown of his head. I was still enjoying my project. Then I moved to the back of his head. My hand with the clippers moved too fast, and before I had a chance to plan my move, I got a little too close to his scalp and made a hole. Bobby jumped.

"Oops," I said.

"Kel! Ow!"

"I didn't mean it."

"Geez!" Bobby said.

"What did you do?" Kevin asked as he came around to the back to look for himself. He started to laugh, which made me laugh.

"It's not funny. What's it look like?" Bobby asked.

"It's fine," I said. "No big deal."

Still giggling, I moved ahead with the clippers to finish the job.

"No way. That's good enough." Bobby stood up.

He wouldn't let me finish that time. But he was able to laugh about it later. All three of us laughed about that story for a long time.

He let me try again with the clippers the next time he came home, and I got better at it. I think we both liked getting rid of that hair. It was a chance to start over. The long, greasy, dirty hair reminded both of us of how far away from home he had been. Cutting it away was the one thing we could do to try and get back to the way it used to be.

We didn't talk much as we left the jail. I tried not to lecture or cry. I didn't want to scare him away.

"Hey, can we go get my stuff?" Bobby asked.

"Sure, where is it? Is it close?"

"At my friend's house, not too far from here." He told me where to turn, and we pulled up in front of a house in what was becoming a familiar neighborhood to me. I sat in my car and waited on the street while he went in the house. Fifteen minutes passed. I started to get restless. I stared at the house, looking for some sign of life, a sign of Bobby. The street was empty. I was sure his stuff would fit in a few plastic bags and couldn't possibly take this long to pack. I sat in my car and waited. A young kid came out of the house and I rolled down my window.

"See Robert in there?" I asked.

"Yeah." I looked at the kid, waiting for more information.

"He just went out the back," the kid mumbled as he walked away.

My mouth dropped open as my fists pounded the steering wheel. *Not again.* My throat swelled, cutting off the air to my chest, threatening to suffocate me. *That bastard.* I didn't understand why he chose this life over our family, his home. He grew up in the same house I did. How could he leave that for this? We took him away from this life; why did he want to stay here?

Bobby had climbed out a back window and down a fire escape to avoid coming home with me that day. I drove around the neighborhood for an hour looking for him, slowly coming to terms with the fact that it's hard to find someone who doesn't want to be found.

Bobby

I'd moved in with Wendy, a friend of my Dad and Ronnie, after I left them in Pennsylvania and hitchhiked back to Binghamton. I helped Wendy and her mom, Sue, with their karaoke business. That was fun. Wendy had a lot of kids. Two living with her and three more next door, living with Sue. Lacey lived with Sue too. She was fourteen or fifteen and babysat the kids. When they needed money for cigarettes or Christmas presents, Sue took Lacey to truck stops and waited while she had sex with guys in the trucks. She would beat Lacey if she didn't do what she told her to do. Sue recruited me to give Lacey rides to the truck stop and wait until she was ready to come home. Sue's glass eye freaked me out. That and the fact she had been in prison for burning down somebody's house. On one of our trips to the truck stop, I was arrested for loitering, which was later reduced to disorderly conduct.

Sue and Wendy were obsessed with lawn ornaments and furniture. The state cops found me one time and questioned me about a set of Seven Dwarfs they had stolen from somebody's front yard. Sue and Wendy had also pulled up in front of a store they'd seen from the highway that had a parking lot full of lawn furniture. I helped them load the truck. I was with them when they were arrested, and I got charged with trespassing.

I finally got enough nerve to move out. I left without any of my things. I was afraid to go back and get my stuff. I called the police station and asked them to help me. I walked over to Sue's house while the cop parked his car in front of her house. I saw my stuff in bags on the porch. They must have heard I was coming. I grabbed the bags and walked to my new apartment while the cop drove away.

Two weeks later, I was sitting on the couch in my new place. I was so glad to be out of Wendy's house and away from Sue bossing me around. I'd wanted to live alone but had a guy staying with me. Hadn't seen him for a couple of days though. He was nice enough. I knew him from the street, knew he got his money selling drugs. His place was just condemned and everybody had to move out. I told him he could stay with me. I knew what it was like to need a place to crash.

I looked around my place. I noticed a loose ceiling tile above me. I got up from the couch, grabbed a chair, and stood on it. I moved the loose tile and found a wallet hidden in the ceiling, looked inside, and counted one hundred and fifty dollars. My roommate must have hid it there before he left town.

I sat back down on the couch, fingering the money in my hands. The twenties, the ten-dollar bills. I looked around my bare apartment with the old, shaggy furniture left by the tenant before me. I wished I'd never come to Binghamton five years ago. Wished I'd never left home. Every time I'd called my sister collect over the last five years, she'd say, Come home. You can stay with me. You don't have to go back to school. You can get your GED, a job. Nobody's mad at you. But it wasn't that easy. Wasn't easy to admit I was wrong. That it wasn't better out here.

I came looking for my real parents. I thought they'd be happy to have the kid back that was taken away so many years ago, that I'd fit in better with them than I did at home. But that didn't happen. Everywhere I went I felt like I wasn't enough. My so-called friends

CHASING THE MERRY-GO-ROUND

only wanted me around because I knew how to drive and would wait for Lacey at the truck stop until she'd earned enough money. And the gang I'd let beat me black and blue so I'd be one of them acted like they didn't know me when the cops came. They let me rot in jail by myself for stealing that stereo until Kelly bailed me out. Someday I'd get my own place, with a garage for my tools and a yard.

I was tired.
Tired of moving—running from place to place.
Tired of not working.
Tired of being a scumbag.
Tired of this life.

I took the money out, put the wallet back in the ceiling, and replaced the tile. I took one last look around and walked out the door. After stopping at Kmart to buy clothes, I went to the bus station and bought a ticket for home.

…nobody's fault

DR. MARSHA AND I WERE IN OUR USUAL POSITIONS. Me: black leather couch, pillow, tissues. Her: legal pad, pen, eyes.

"I'm concerned about your self-blame," she said.

"What do you mean?" I asked.

"I see a pattern with you, and I think your self-blame is getting in the way of your anger and sadness that you should be feeling."

"I'm not here to blame my parents for anything if that's where you're going with this," I said.

My parents were two of the best people I knew. For most of my childhood, my dad left for work at four thirty in the morning, six days a week. He was foreman of a gravel pit for twenty years. Long before "Take Our Daughters to Work Day" was launched, my father would take my sisters and me to the gravel pit with him once or twice a summer. The three of us girls would race to his pickup truck with sleep still in our eyes, fighting for the best seat—the one right next to Dad where we could shift the truck into gear with our small hands on the stick shift and his calloused hand on top. The dust-covered dash, his work gloves and hardhat stored behind the seat, the grimy chains and cables on the floor, and the cab of the truck thick with the smell of dirt, sweat, and grease—his truck was his world, and I loved being in it. After stopping at the diner for donuts, we hopped out of the truck and stepped up into the office trailer to say hi to the guys before they went out to start their day. We hung out in the trailer eating butterscotch candies the dispatcher kept in the desk drawer until it was our turn to sit on Dad's lap while he ran the backhoe, bulldozer, or dump truck. When the workday was done, we hopped back in his truck for the ride home; we all took an oath not to tell our mother we'd eaten an ice cream cone before dinner.

When that job ended abruptly, my dad picked up milk from farms and delivered it to dairies, loaded trucks at a warehouse, and then hauled a UPS tandem tractor-trailer for a season. He did whatever he needed to do to support and feed us. Then he started and ran his own construction business for another twenty years, working harder than ever. My dad came to as many of my field hockey games and track meets as he could. When he wasn't working, he was home or at church. He played with us in the swimming pool instead of golfing on Saturdays, and watched TV and ate popcorn and ice cream with us on Friday night instead of playing poker with the guys. He was there. He loved us with everything he had.

At fifty-five years old, my dad sold his construction business, and he and my mother became ordained ministers and began working for their church. He built a new career of being present at the most important moments of people's lives. With my mother at his side, they baptized babies and counseled couples before marriage and again if their marriage was struggling. Together, they visited the old and sick and performed hundreds of weddings and funerals. Their mission was to love people any way they could, and people loved them back. Once they found God at Camp Aldersgate in 1975, they never looked back. Their faith, unconditional love, and compassion inspired everyone they met. They had worked hard and sacrificed for our family. How could I blame them for anything?

"It's not about blaming them either, Kelly," Dr. Marsha said. She was not impressed with my testimony about my parents.

"They sound like lovely people," she said, "but the things you've told me about your early years tell a different story."

I started to interrupt and she held a hand up.

"Let me finish."

She continued on with her theory, which began to make sense to me as she talked. I had been consumed with figuring out what it was about me that allowed Kevin to do this to me. For many years, I blamed myself for all of Bobby's problems. I blamed myself when my sisters' marriages fell apart and they were self-destructing. I agonized over their decisions and unhappiness. I thought if I could do the right thing, say the right thing, then they would in turn do the right thing. Somehow I had convinced myself that their burdens were not only mine but were my fault. I had always carried the weight of everyone's emotions and potential unhappiness. If the people around me were unhappy or dysfunctional, then there must be something wrong with me. I must not be good enough, pretty enough, witty enough, or smart enough. I had spent too many days being unhappy and miserable because of what was going on in other people's lives.

Dr. Marsha was right. I needed to stop this cycle of assuming everything was my fault or caused by some deficiency in me. I was so intent on not blaming my father or husband for anything that I rested all the blame on my own shoulders. I realized that for many years I blamed myself for Bobby's struggles. If I had been a better sister, Bobby wouldn't have run away from home. Why did I have to blame anybody? *How much of my life had I wasted with burdens that weren't mine to bear?*

NOMAD

FIFTEEN. FIFTEEN IN TEN YEARS. WAS THAT POSSIBLE? I ran through the list, counting on my fingers the ramshackle rooms and dingy apartments Bobby had lived in since he had boarded that bus in Binghamton and moved back home in 1996, ten years ago. He'd had almost as many jobs as apartments and was working toward having as many cars. He also had an ex-wife and an eight-year-old daughter. I could see in my rearview mirror that the white Pontiac with the busted front axle, yet another car in the trail of failed intentions to keep Bobby independent, was on its last leg as he followed us to the John Milton Inn.

The John Milton Inn had a nice ring to it—perhaps an old fashioned inn, nestled on a quiet street lined on both sides with majestic oak trees, named for a literary figure, with a large porch for guests to sip iced tea in the afternoons, bedrooms filled with antique furniture and white lace bed covers. This John Milton Inn resembled none of that. It sat on the edge of a busy traffic circle in an old industrial section of Syracuse. The inn's best features were that I could rent Bobby a room for a few weeks without a lease, and it was a short drive to Embassy Suites where he worked in housekeeping.

The John Milton Inn was tan with brown trim; its name in red letters ran across the front of the building. The red painted curbs were chipped and peeling. Instead of a porch, guests sat outside their rooms in lawn chairs with coolers by their sides, music thumping out of radios while they cooked dinner on old charcoal grills. We stood in the parking lot for a few minutes before we ventured inside, putting off what neither one of us wanted. I warned Bobby about the kind of people who stayed in places where rooms were rented by the hour. I told him he would see hookers and their pimps, junkies and their dealers. I told him to stay away from the high school parties— two hundred kids in one room and all the alcohol they could afford. I knew from his years on the streets of Binghamton that he had a tendency to gravitate toward people who were nothing but trouble. He was an easy target for them. He promised me he would keep to himself—eat, sleep, and go to work. How did we end up here?

Ten years ago, I was relieved when Bobby finally came home. I thought that was the answer, the solution. Those five years he was gone, I thought all I had to do was get him home. The rest would fall into place. He would get a job, an apartment, his GED, then tackle a trade of some sort and begin his life of adulthood. Self-sufficient. Safe. Normal. On the merry-go-round with the rest of us.

But the reality was that he still lived like a nomad. For the last ten years, he had wandered from place to place without settling anywhere. Bobby didn't have a problem finding a place to live. I never worried about him finding a job. He could find minimum-wage employment easy enough. The problem was he kept losing them— apartments and jobs—and we'd have to start all over again, going in circles, always ending up at the same place it seemed.

He was twenty-one when he first moved home. He slept on our couch for a few months; I was happy to have him. I didn't mind his dirty socks on my living room floor or his bike flopped on its side in my front yard. I didn't mind that my living room had turned into his bedroom and my only couch was messy with blankets and pillows. I liked knowing where he was at the end of each day when night fell.

Eager to work and earn his own money, Bobby signed up with a temporary staffing agency, and they got him a job at a company that produced silk-screened T-shirts. It was close enough to my house that he could ride his bike back and forth to the shop. I was as hesitant as I was excited. I still worried that some morning I would get up and find the couch empty, his duffel bag gone, with him on a bus back to Binghamton. But that didn't happen. He stayed this time, and after a few months passed, I relaxed a little bit. Took a breath.

It wasn't surprising that before too long he met a girl. They met on a summer night at a balloon festival in the next town over from us. Bobby told me that she had asked him out that night. They became a couple almost instantly. She was younger than he was and had quit school in ninth grade. Even though I worried she wasn't good for him, I was glad he had a girlfriend here. One more thing to keep him in town. One more thing to keep him settled.

Bobby moved into an apartment on Canal Street with the help of Kevin and my parents. We moved his old bed in, an old couch from my parents, and gathered up some dishes and pots and pans. Kevin gave him a set of stereo speakers. They were big—three feet tall, two feet wide and weighed forty pounds each. Bobby loved them. He wrapped them in strands of Christmas lights that year. Of course, in a matter of days, his girlfriend moved in. I didn't panic. Again, I thought that would settle him. Job—check. Apartment—check. My plan seemed to be working.

Until the T-shirt factory fired him.

"Bo-ob! What happened?" I asked. I paced around my dining room with the phone to my ear.

"I was late. Just a couple of times though."

"Why?"

"I didn't wake up."

"What about your alarm clock?"

"I set it. I think Annie turned it off."

"What? Why would she do that?"

"She didn't want me to leave her." Oh, young love. Young love made me want to vomit and throw the phone at him.

"What's your plan?"

"I'll get another job. It'll be okay. Relax."

"It's not that easy, Bob. You don't have a high school diploma. We need to look into getting your GED."

Not long after he lost his job, the landlord asked them to move out. I never really heard the full story. The neighbors were complaining. They were too loud. It didn't matter the reason. They were out. Apartment—gone. Job—gone. So much for my plan.

They moved into the small trailer of Annie's dad, and Bobby paid rent to sleep on the floor. He got a new job at Walmart. I exhaled again. Walmart is a good company. He could work there for years. He could move up the ladder. Maybe they would pay for his GED. He could retire from Walmart. He worked at the McDonald's inside the store, then in the deli, and then as an overnight stocker. When sleeping on the floor of the trailer got old, he moved out.

Bobby moved back into my parents' house for a few months without Annie. I thought my parents could keep tabs on him, make sure he was getting to work. But deep down I knew this living arrangement wouldn't last long. Even though time healed most of the wounds inflicted before he had run away, he and my mother were simply incompatible as housemates.

Kevin and I were still in the house we had moved into right after I finished college. It was a small two-bedroom one-story ranch. The second bedroom doubled as my office and the room where Kevin's boys stayed when they were with us on weekends. I didn't have an extra room for Bobby.

Bobby moved into the old Five Corners Tavern, across the street from Walmart. Since his only mode of transportation was his bike, I thought this was a good idea. The old bar was now separated into rooms that were rented out. His one-room apartment was in the back, just big enough for a bed, a dresser, and his girlfriend. But that place didn't last either, and for reasons I'm unsure of, they moved out.

Bobby and Annie moved to an apartment on Williams Street. This apartment was unremarkable, and the only reason I remember it is because it's where they lived when I found out Annie was pregnant. I don't remember how I found out. I don't remember if they told me or if I noticed her expanding stomach or if I realized it when Bobby told me she had been getting sick in the mornings. What I do remember is a moment of panic. This wasn't part of the plan. Bobby had yet to prove he could take care of himself. How would he take care of a baby? He was twenty-two, had been home about a year, and had lived four different places—not counting my couch. Even though I was overwhelmed by the thought of yet another person to keep safe, to keep tabs on, to keep—there was a part of me that thought maybe this was just the thing he needed to settle down, to get focused, to get his GED. The apartment on Williams Street wasn't big enough to fit a crib, so they moved out.

Bobby moved into a larger apartment on Madison Street. On a ninety-five degree day, with the sun blazing and humidity peaking, Kevin and I parked the U-Haul I had rented in front of the old building. It was then that Bobby told us their new apartment was on the fourth floor.

"Bob. Do you really think the fourth floor is a good idea?" I asked.

He shrugged his shoulders.

"Annie's pregnant. How's she going to do that when she has a baby?"

He looked at me with a blank stare.

Bobby and Annie stood on the sidewalk smoking cigarettes while I trudged up the stairs with the small items. Kevin and my father carried Bobby's bed and dressers, his tables and chairs, and the crib I helped them find, up those four longer, steeper flights of stairs characteristic of old buildings, and swore that this would be the last time they'd move him. Bobby grabbed a few things here and there and carried them up, but mostly Kevin, my dad, and I just stepped around Bobby and Annie. I could have let them move everything in themselves, but I figured we would do it faster. And the faster I settled him in this new place, the sooner I could go home and salvage what was left of my weekend.

Bobby became a father on June 6, 1998. I went to the hospital to meet my new niece and to hold her. She was small, six pounds, tightly swaddled in her blanket, with light hair and soft skin, just like her father had when I first met him. She had his wide cheeks and upturned nose. She would turn out to be an easy baby, an easy toddler, and would grow into an irreplaceable young girl—sweet, friendly, with a smile and a kind word for everyone—a shining light I could not imagine our family without. As I held her that first day, I inhaled her newborn freshness, her sweetness. I kissed her cheeks and nose. I made promises. *It's going to be okay, Mersadies. It's all going to be okay.* I don't know if I was reassuring her or me.

Bobby and Annie moved again when it became too much to trudge up four floors with the baby and groceries. Lenox Avenue was a little easier to move into since it was the second story of a house. Despite their promise that they would never help again, Kevin and my father emptied the Madison Street apartment, down those four flights of long, steep stairs, into another rented U-Haul and traipsed everything to Lenox Avenue. The landlord there was good to Bobby. He would take weekly payments on the rent and let them catch up when their tax refund came.

I stopped in every week to check on the baby and make sure she was eating and was clean, make sure they had diapers and formula. One day while Bobby was watching her, he fell asleep, and she rolled underneath the Christmas tree. She was fine and didn't get hurt. I reminded him that if he was tired and felt sleepy, he needed to put her in the crib or baby seat, where at least she couldn't roll away.

Bobby quit his job at Walmart to go to work for a roofing company not long after they moved to Lenox Avenue. The pay was better, and he had always dreamt of working construction like our dad. The first couple of days were good; he cleaned up the job site and stacked the bundles of shingles for the guys. On the third day, the guys were working up on a roof of a two-story house. The boss asked him to bring up a bundle of shingles. Bobby picked up a bundle and started to climb up the ladder like he had seen the other guys do. It was a lot harder than he thought to carry the shingles with one hand and hold on to the ladder with the other. They were heavy. The

103

higher he went on the ladder, the shakier his legs became. Looking up at the slanted roof made his knees buckle. He reached out with his other hand, the hand holding the shingles, to grab the side of the ladder, and the bundle of shingles smashed to the ground. He climbed down quickly after them, relieved to be heading in the other direction. The boss yelled at him, "If you can't handle it, go home." Bobby took his pay for the three days he worked, went home, and called me.

"What do you mean you quit Walmart?" I stood up from my desk and held the phone away from my mouth while I screamed on the inside. "I thought you liked it there. That was a good job."

"I always wanted to work in construction. I didn't know it would be so hard."

"You're afraid of heights. What did you think was going to happen?"

"Yeah, I know. I didn't think I'd have to climb a ladder."

"You never think. You can't do stuff like that anymore. You have a baby." I'm sure Bobby had tuned me out at that point, but I kept talking. "Did you call that 1-800 number I gave you about a GED? Bob? Are you listening?"

Walmart filled his job right away so he couldn't go back there, and unemployment wasn't enough to pay the rent for his apartment. They moved out of Lenox Avenue.

Bobby moved into a room behind some pool hall. Annie and the baby moved back to her dad's trailer. Annie slept on the couch, and the baby slept in her bassinet. Bobby didn't stay at the pool hall long; he thought the place was creepy. He joined Annie and the baby at her dad's and slept on the floor again.

He got a job as a dishwasher at a Denny's restaurant and a second job at McDonald's. He was almost twenty-five now. I worried about him turning thirty, then forty, then fifty and still working as a cart pusher or dishwasher. How would he support himself and his family? Working forty hours per week at minimum wage is just enough to keep you from qualifying for assistance but not nearly enough to live on.

Bobby found another place to live and moved to Walnut Street. He had called his old landlord from Lenox Avenue and asked if he had a place for him. Walnut Street was half a house. It had two bedrooms upstairs and leaned dramatically to one side, like it was ready to tip over at any time. Their little family settled into this place for almost two years. Bobby got a job at the casino on the nearby Indian reservation as a beverage porter. They were an important employer in the area. He could move up the ladder here. Earn more than minimum wage. Support his family. He could retire from there.

Bobby had been using his bike to get around for the last few years, but to be truly independent he needed a driver's license. Kevin and I were first on the list to call for groceries, emergency trips to the drug store, doctor's appointments, and anything else that came up. My parents also helped and so did Bobby's father-in-law. I tried to get Bobby and Annie to plan their trips to the grocery store, to make lists of what they needed ahead of time, and to check with us before they made doctor's appointments. But they weren't the best planners, which could be very frustrating. One night, I was working late when Kevin got a phone call.

"Hey, Kev. Where's Kelly?"

"Working. Why? What's up, Bob?"

"Um, I uh, uh, need a ride to the store."

"Right now?"

"Yeah."

"It's seven o'clock and snowing. Wait 'til tomorrow."

"I can't. It's sorta an emergency."

"What emergency? What exactly do you need?"

"Woman stuff."

"What?"

"Annie's got her monthly."

"Are you shittin' me?"

"No."

"Tell her to use a dish towel or wash cloth." Kevin slammed the phone down. I imagine he paced around the house for a few minutes, spouting off about Bobby and his inconsiderate lack of planning and selfishness before he begrudgingly picked up the phone to call him back.

"Tell me exactly what she needs. I'll stop at the store on my way to your place." Kevin wrote down the brand name and the size of the pad she wanted, and twenty minutes later, he stood in the middle of the store aisle, overwhelmed by all the choices, trying to find exactly what she wanted, still sputtering about how inconsiderate and selfish they were. By the time I got home, Kevin had calmed down and was able to laugh while he told me the story. I silently thanked God for a man who did things like that when nobody was watching. In the years to come, Kevin and I would have many problems, ones that would seriously challenge our marriage, and it would be nights like this that I would remember. When things happened that otherwise would have driven me away from him, I remembered the way he treated my brother.

Bobby took the written test for his driver's license in 2001; he was twenty-six years old at the time. He and Annie had been participating in a community program designed to support people with young children and limited resources. This organization would occasionally give them rides to doctors' visits and the grocery store. A woman from this program tutored him for the written test. Bobby met her at the library once a week. He took the written test and failed the first time.

"It's okay. No big deal," I told him. "You can take it again."

"That's why I never took it. I was afraid I'd fail," he confessed.

"You can do it. I know you can. A lot of people don't pass the first time. Don't give up, Bob. You'll get it."

He didn't give up. He kept meeting with the tutor at the library. I found out he could have the test questions read to him. A few months later, Kevin took Bobby to the DMV and waited while a worker read him the test questions. This time he passed.

The next step was the driving test. Bobby had driven cars before, so he knew the basics and the mechanics, but he didn't know the rules of the road. A friend he worked with at the casino taught him how to drive, how to execute a three-point turn, and to parallel park. I had been pushing him for five years, and he had been afraid he couldn't do it for five years, but Bobby passed the road test the first time with his friend's car.

His first car was a used Pontiac that he bought for $1000 with his tax refund. We were finally making progress. Job—check. Apartment—check. License—check. His own car—check.

Right after he bought the car, he moved out of the leaning house on Walnut Street. Bobby, Annie, and their four-year old daughter moved into a duplex. While it was yet another move, this time it felt like a good move. My sister and her second husband had bought this duplex as a rental home on Florida Road. It had three bedrooms with a living room and kitchen—the nicest place Bobby had lived since he ran away from my parents' home at sixteen. Bobby applied for HUD assistance, and because they only qualified for a two-bedroom, they moved the dining room table into the third bedroom to convince the inspector that it was, in fact, only a two-bedroom.

It also had a basement, a yard, and a deck. Bobby made a deal with my brother-in-law to mow the lawn and do some painting and other maintenance in exchange for reduced rent. My brother-in-law didn't have to worry about the daily maintenance, and Bobby felt like he owned the place. It seemed perfect.

Less than a month after he bought his first car, Bobby was driving to his new apartment on Florida Road and had to make a left turn in front of oncoming traffic. It was a double lane divided highway. He timed the turn wrong and was hit by a car moving too fast to stop in time. A neighbor towed the Pontiac to the junkyard. Despite my parents' growing frustration with Bobby and his seeming inability to make good choices, they helped out when they could. My father bought him a used black Pontiac Grand Am. Bobby managed to keep this car for a few months, but my dad was worried about it for winter driving so he sold it and bought him a used minivan.

Bobby quit his job at the casino. He loved working there, but now it was a forty-five minute commute and the gas took most of his paycheck. He got a job at another Walmart close to his new apartment. He started as a cart pusher, those guys who corral the way-ward carts in the parking lot and bring them back up to the stalls in the front of the store. He then was promoted to overnight stocker, working nights. He worked there for more than a year, but eventually had to leave because he couldn't regulate his sleep habits successfully to work the overnight shift. He was falling asleep at work. So he went to work for Little Caesars making pizza.

"Bob. You're twenty-six years old. You've got to earn more than minimum wage," I said.

"I know."

"We need to seriously look at that GED program."

"What if I can't do it?"

"You can. I know you're scared. I believe in you." I crossed my fingers, wishing he would believe in himself like I did. If only it were that easy.

It wasn't long after Bobby moved into the duplex on Florida Road, that he buried his biological father, George. It was on a June morning in 2001—with sun that was warm and bright, too bright it seemed to bury someone—that we huddled in a half circle around his grave. He was buried at Lenox Rural Cemetery next to my grandmother. We all came to pay our respects: my parents, Kevin, my brother and his wife, my sister and her second husband, my other sister, Bobby and his wife and her dad, and of course, Ronnie. My mother's older brother and his wife were also there. George was sixty-three when he died, his life and habits finally winning the war for his body and soul. Bobby was twenty-six.

George and Ronnie had moved to Oneida, New York, from Binghamton about six or seven months before he died. They had arrived in a U-Haul with everything they owned in the truck, including seven or eight dogs. They lived in the back, along with the animals. At night, they would park the truck in a shopping plaza parking lot to sleep. Animal control eventually came and rescued the dogs. George and Ronnie saved their welfare checks until they had enough money to get an apartment. Bobby had kept in touch with his dad. They had spoken on the phone once or twice a year in the six years that had passed since Bobby left Binghamton. Bobby told me he wouldn't have cared if he ever saw or heard from Ronnie again, but he had wanted to stay in touch with his father.

Bobby

I still couldn't believe my father was gone. We had just gone to Walmart together to buy groceries three days ago. I liked helping him; I felt sorry for him. He had been sick for a long time. The day before he died, I talked to him on the phone. He seemed okay. I was working the overnight shift at Walmart the night Ronnie called. She told me that George couldn't breathe. She was taking him to the emergency room. I finished my shift and went home and went to bed. Annie woke me up a few hours later. The hospital called. George wanted to see me.

I stood next to his hospital bed and held his hand. "Robert, can you cover me up?" He whispered so softly that I could barely hear him over the machines beeping and buzzing and his own wheezing and fighting to breathe.

I pulled a blanket off the empty bed next to him and added it to the blankets he was already covered with. My father was shivering and couldn't get warm.

"Can you make sure to get my check and pay my bills?" he asked. "I don't want Ronnie to take all my money." I didn't tell my father that Ronnie had already taken the money from his bank account. He wasn't dead yet and she had spent it.

"I think I saw angels shutting off my oxygen," he told me. I didn't tell my father that his oxygen levels were too high when he arrived at the hospital, as if it had been turned up on purpose, dangerous for someone who had respiratory failure and chronic lung disease. I thought Ronnie might have been the "angel."

I held his hand. "It's going to be all right, Dad," I told him.

After he fell asleep, me and Annie went to the waiting room. The nurse woke us up out of a nap after midnight. "He's taken a turn for the worse," she said. "I'm afraid he's taking his last couple of breaths." I called my parents; they rushed to the hospital and prayed with George. He died at four o'clock that morning. I lost my dad for good that time.

"Let not your heart be troubled," my father read from John 14:1 as he performed the graveside service. He told us that the body returns to the earth from which it came; earth to earth, ashes to ashes, dust to dust.

He talked about George as a young man, what he was like when my father first met him. "And God will wipe away every tear from their eyes; there shall be no more death, nor sorrow, nor crying. There shall be no more pain, for the former things have passed away" (Rev. 21:4).

After my father finished, I read a poem I had written.

Amazing grace took you from this place
and gave you a second chance,
now is the life you were meant to live,
now is your time to dance.

At the end of the ceremony, we sang "Amazing Grace." *Amazing Grace how sweet the sound that saved a wretch like me!* We read the words of the hymn from papers I had copied that morning and handed to everyone when it was time. My alto voice and my father's baritone were strong and clear, carrying the chorus of reluctant voices, determined to honor the life we were burying. *I once was lost, but now am found, was blind, but now I see.*

By the third verse, Bobby broke. His knees buckled as he sobbed while my father held him up. Each sob carried the sadness of never really knowing his father. He believed George would have been different without Ronnie around. He once told me that he regretted ever meeting them and regretted that his father didn't try to visit him more when he was a little boy. "I'm sure he had stuff to do," he told me.

We kept singing while my mother cried for the man who was once the boy she grew up with; she cried for her brother. I'm sure she remembered the fresh face of a young boy she laughed with, played with, argued with, the older brother she followed around, the one she helped with his paper route. I'm sure she remembered his eyes when they were still sober and hopeful.

And I cried. I cried for Bobby and for my mother. I cried because I was afraid. Afraid that Bobby was just like his father, in more ways than his short legs, brown eyes, and wide nose. Afraid that despite everything I did or didn't do, or how much I loved him, or how hard I fought against it, Bobby would end up just like him and I couldn't stop it. Afraid that he would end up living in a U-Haul in a Walmart parking lot and dying too young.

Despite the sadness of that day, Bobby was happy living in the duplex on Florida Road. He thought they were all happy. They liked the backyard the most at that place. Mersadies loved to play on the swing set and run around with the neighbor kids even though they were all older than her. Bobby became friends with his neighbors. One of them was a member of the Hinsdale Fire Department and he asked Bobby to join. He completed a couple of training classes, but he couldn't pass the written tests. He couldn't pass the physical tests either, but they let him hang around anyway and ride along on calls. Every Tuesday night he looked forward to the meetings.

Bobby mostly watched while they were trained on cutting open car doors and fighting fires. He did get to help cook when they had pancake breakfasts. Hanging out with the guys at the fire department would always be one of his favorite things about living there, and when he eventually moves away, he will miss it. At the house on Florida Road, for the first time in a long time, Bobby was really happy—until his wife decided she didn't want to be married to him anymore.

Bobby

I walked in the door after work and noticed right away that something was different. Pictures were missing. Pictures of me and Annie. I got a sick feeling in my stomach. She'd been acting weird for a while. She left the house at midnight sometimes and didn't tell me where she was going. She'd been late to her babysitting job. She came home one day with a black eye, and I didn't believe her story on how she got it. How do you run into a cupboard? I didn't know how it happened, but I knew she was lying.

I found out the guy's name from my daughter. She was four years old. One day, I asked where they'd been, and she said, "Swimmin' at Ryan's." I drove around the neighborhood I thought they might be in and saw her car. Then I knew where Ryan lived. One Friday, Annie's brother picked Annie and Mersadies up in his car; they were going to stay at his place for the weekend. I called to talk to my daughter and asked where Mommy was. "She's at Ryan's." Annie's brother grabbed the phone away from her before she could say anything else.

So I knew. Just like I knew before we got married. When we lived in that apartment on Williams Street and she came home wearing another guy's jacket.

And today all the pictures were gone. She was home when I got there; she had one of her friends with her.

"Where are the pictures?" I asked.

"Oh, I took those down to clean 'em."

I knew she was lying. It was hard to look at her. Then she said something that broke my heart.

"Bob, I love Ryan."

I couldn't talk. Even though I knew she'd been with somebody else, I wasn't expecting her to love him. Then I said the words that would change my life and I'd regret. "If you're gonna be with him, you're gonna move out." As soon as the words left my mouth, I wished I could take them back. But it was too late. She left that night.

I thought about the night I met her at the Balloon Fest seven years ago when I was staying on Kelly's couch. How she came over to me and said, "Hey. You wanna come over?" I rode my bike to her dad's. We'd been together ever since. I thought about all the places we'd lived, everything we'd been through. I thought about the day we found out she was pregnant, afraid to tell anybody; we knew we'd get yelled at for being irresponsible. I was scared and amazed at the same time. I was gonna be a father. We were both scared shitless. And then, when Mersadies was born, we were afraid to hold her at first, afraid we couldn't take care of her. But we did. We knew we'd never hit her, and we didn't. We'd done all right with her, not perfect, but all right. She was doing okay.

I stayed in the apartment for a while. I couldn't work full-time and take care of my daughter. I tried for a few months. But it was hard to get her up in the morning and on the bus; to make sure she had breakfast and supper at night. It was hard to keep up on the laundry and to figure out what she should wear to school. And when I just couldn't do it anymore, I called Annie and asked her to take her.

And she did. I was all by myself in the three-bedroom apartment on Florida Road. I couldn't afford it for long. HUD wouldn't help me anymore once they found out I was alone in a three-bedroom.

I missed Mersadies. I saw her on some weekends, but it wasn't enough. It wasn't what I wanted. All I wanted was to give her a good life. I wanted to give her a home.

A one-room apartment in the back of a retail store on North Main Street would be Bobby's next home. It was a small room, perfectly square, with white walls and no windows except for the eight-by-twelve window in the steel door. He had lived there a little more than a month when I realized it had been too long since I had heard from him. On Saturday morning, I went to his apartment and knocked on the door.

"Bob?" No answer. I knocked a few more times, calling his name again.

"You in there?" I found something to stand on and peeked in the small window in the door. His place was empty. The small, square room was bare. He later told me he felt trapped in that place and had to get out.

By this time, cell phones were everywhere, and I always made sure Bobby had one that was working. I tracked him down in a nearby town, twenty minutes away. He was renting a bedroom from a guy he met through the fire department. He didn't stay there long, said the guy was always trying to touch him and grab him. "He was weird." Bobby packed up his belongings after a month or two, put everything he owned in storage, and left to stay with his friend, Shawna. She said he could sleep on her couch for a while.

He was working at Walmart for a third time when he met Shawna. He unloaded trucks at the loading dock. One day, she asked him to take a push lawn mower to her house. She didn't have a car and he did. She convinced him it was paid for, that someone bought it for her. Bobby pushed the lawn mower out the front door of the store, loaded it in his van, and took it to her house. The next day, the store manager called Bobby into his office. He and the loss prevention team drilled Bobby with questions about the lawn mower and other things that were missing from the electronics department and other places in the store. He told them he was doing a favor for a friend and that she said it was paid for. They fired Bobby on the spot. He was the one who walked the mower out of the store; he was guilty.

After that is when I started looking for a place for him to live. I began to realize that whatever I thought I was doing to help him was not working. The last ten years he had wandered from apartment to apartment, job to job, car after wrecked car, bad decision after bad decision.

Bobby got a job at the Mobil station. The guy who owned the pawnshop next door asked Bobby to trade him his minivan for his Ford Taurus. Although my dad had bought the van, Bobby made the trade without checking with my dad, or anybody else. He thought his van was having problems, so he made the trade. Two weeks later, he was driving to a friend's house when smoke billowed out from under the hood of his newly traded car. The transmission blew up; that was the end of the Ford Taurus. That's when he gave a cashier at the Mobil one hundred dollars for the white Pontiac with the busted front axle.

So there we were. The John Milton Inn was the last stop—after ten years of apartments, jobs, and cars, after all the failed attempts at convincing Bobby to think before he acted, to think before he trusted, to remember what happened the last time he did this or that—this place was the last place I thought we'd be. The last place I wanted to be.

A small lobby sat in the middle of the building with a long row of rooms down each side. A man in an undershirt sat at the desk and took our credit card. Kevin asked for a second floor room. We thought it would be safer to be one level up from the pimps and dealers in the parking lot.

We walked down the dimly lit hallway. Voices leaked through the thin walls. We found Bobby's room and unlocked the door. The mattress was covered in plastic, the carpet and bedspread were stained, the air was musty and stale. We had already been to the grocery store and bought him cups of chili and noodles that could be cooked in the small microwave in his room. When he got home from work, he would lock himself in his room, close the drapes, and stay there until he had to go to work again, hoping none of his neighbors would bother him. He would only venture out for the free coffee and donuts in the lobby every morning. After we got him settled, we left.

Bobby was thirty years old. Yet, I felt like I was leaving behind a little boy to fend for himself in this dark, desperate place, surrounded by people who didn't know him or care about him. As Kevin and I merged onto the traffic circle and drove away from the John Milton Inn, I made myself two promises—that I would get Bobby out of there as soon as possible and that I would never let him end up in a place like that again.

After all those years of thinking I had all the answers, I knew that day I was wrong.

THE WAY HE IS

I KEPT MY PROMISE TO BOBBY AND DIDN'T LEAVE HIM AT the John Milton Inn for very long. It took about two weeks to find an apartment for him. I signed the lease and agreed to write the monthly rent check. Bobby agreed to give me his unemployment check to cover it. I would be the primary contact with the landlord. This was my way of ensuring he didn't get evicted for not paying his rent or for some other reason. It also made certain that he didn't just pack up and move to some friend's couch. In the past, I had always tried to work with Bobby. I thought I could lecture him into the right decision, explain him into doing the right thing. I wanted *him* to do it. But I realized that day at the John Milton Inn that what I had been trying with Bobby wasn't working.

Not long after he moved into his new apartment, I was at an ordinary Sunday dinner at my mother's house, talking about Bobby to my younger sister, Patti, who was an RN. "He reminds me of one of my patients with fetal alcohol," she casually said to me.

"What do you mean?" I asked.

"I have a patient with fetal alcohol syndrome. He reminds me a lot of Bobby."

I still wasn't sure what she meant, but I was interested in anything that might help me understand Bobby better. I went to my mother's bedroom, sat at her computer desk, and searched for fetal alcohol syndrome on the Internet. In a matter of minutes, I found the characteristics of an adult with FAS. I read the list. *It was Bobby.* My heart beat fast. My mouth dried up.

"Dinner's ready," my mother called from the dining room.

I couldn't move from my seat.

"Coming," I yelled back, but I couldn't take my eyes off what I was reading yet.

Bobby's life was playing in slow motion in my mind as I read.

Mild facial abnormalities—small eye openings, flattened middle of face, flattened groove in area between nose and upper lip

I thought about the day Bobby had come home from school at seven or eight years old and asked me why he had Chinese eyes. A kid in his class had asked him that day if he was full of Chinese. His eyes were narrow. He later told me he hated his slanted eyes. Not only had he been in the special class, but he also looked different when all he wanted was to be like everybody else.

A speech impediment as a child

I heard Bobby's toddler voice saying "I yuh you" when he said goodnight, or "yee me yone" when we were bothering him. I thought of how my sister and I still trade "wha you ben doey?"/"oh, nutty mut" when we call each other on the phone.

Poor judgment, unable to cope with stress, poor memory, disorganization, poor comprehension, poor problem-solving skills

I thought of the phone calls when he described the position of the long hand and the small hand on the clock so I could tell him what time it was.

Difficulty finding and keeping a job

The T-shirt factory, three different Walmarts, the roofing job, McDonald's, the Mobil station, making pizzas, dish washing, cart pushing.

Trouble with expressing thoughts, self-esteem, time management, following directions

Bobby called me frequently to read me the cooking instructions on the back of a cake mix or a recipe for spaghetti sauce, and we would work through which measuring cup to use or whether or not he had a nine-inch pan. He would spell me the words he didn't know.

Struggle with budgeting and spending of money

I had tried to teach him how to use a checking account, explaining how you have to have money in your account to cover every check before you write it. Once, Bobby wrote a check to Walmart to pay for his groceries for more than the amount in his checking account; the check bounced. Walmart called him and told him he was on the bad-check list and that he could be arrested for writing bad checks. Not only was he unable to write any more checks, he was also unable to return anything to Walmart for a refund until he paid the balance and the bounced check fee. He was embarrassed that they thought he was writing bad checks on purpose and afraid he could get arrested next time, so he gave up on ever having his own checking account.

Naïve and easily taken advantage of by unscrupulous people

I remembered the petty crimes Bobby had been arrested for after "friends" convinced him to steal a car stereo from Kmart and lawn ornaments from a stranger's front lawn and to drive the teenage prostitute to the truck stop. I thought about his "friend" Shawna and the job he recently lost at Walmart because she convinced him to walk out the front door with a lawn mower.

And just recently, he'd lost what would be his last car. It was another Pontiac, a tan Grand Prix. A week or so after it happened, Bobby called me at home. "Hey. Somebody stole my car," he said in a very nonchalant and casual way, as if he called me every day to tell me his car had been stolen.

"What do you mean somebody stole your car? Who?" I demanded. I turned off the TV and paced my living room.

"I dunno."

"Did you call the police?"

"No, they called me," Bobby said, as if this was completely normal.

I could feel the heat of my blood pressure rising and fought to keep my voice level.

"That doesn't make any sense," I said. "Where are you?"

"Home."

"Where was your car?"

"Parked in my parking lot."

"Were the keys in it?"

"No."

"Well, then how did someone steal it?"

"It was these two kids."

"What two kids?"

"Shawna's younger brother and a friend."

"How did they get the keys?"

After twenty minutes of interrogation, I finally got his version of the story. Shawna's brother and a friend had gone to Bobby's new apartment to watch movies. Bobby fell asleep. A neighbor woke him up some time later and told him two kids had just taken off with his car. The thieves hit a guardrail and wrecked it. They were attempting to drive the car home when the police pulled them over. The car was towed to a junkyard. But the details didn't really matter. Another car was gone. Another "friend" had burned him. I was furious, just like all the other times something like this happened.

Neurological problems, sleep disorders

Bobby first experienced cataplexy when he worked at the casino. One night, while holding a tray of drinks, his legs gave out, and he fell to his knees, the tray of drinks spilling all over him and the floor. I didn't think much of it until it happened again when we were at my mother's house for dinner. He laughed at something someone said and fell against the dryer. And then it happened again when we were playing kickball. It was his turn to run, and instead, his legs collapsed and he fell to the ground. I researched those episodes and his propensity to sleep when he was talking, having dinner, and riding in a car, and I became convinced that Bobby had narcolepsy. I had yet to get a doctor to diagnose him.

Dental problems

Bobby had been losing his teeth over the past few years and had now lost so many that it was difficult to understand him, especially on the phone.

Learning disability—lower than normal IQ

I remembered the night on the phone, not so long ago, when he rambled on and on about Martina McBride's new song but then had to hang up suddenly. "I gotta go. I wanna get the coloring book before Mersadies finishes all the good pictures." I had ignored the fact that he not only still collected Matchbox cars and Hess Trucks but he still lay on the floor and played with them. I had ignored the fact that he did all these things while also being a man who knew how to fix televisions and CD players, go to work, and take care of his daughter. I had ignored the many ways that he was still a little boy inside the body of a thirty-year-old man.

Later that night, after dinner was finished at my mother's, I continued my research. Over the next few days I bought and read two books, *The Broken Cord* by Michael Dorris and *Damaged Angels* by Bonnie Buxton. I marked passages with tabs and highlighted paragraphs that spoke to me about Bobby. Buxton wrote that FAS is often referred to as an invisible disability. Adults with FAS often appear "normal," at least compared to other mentally disabled people, and their disability is often disregarded.

In her book, Buxton quotes Dr. Sterling Clarren, from the University of Washington, saying, "The person with FAS will always need an 'external forebrain.'" There was a name for what I had become! Buxton explained that the adult with FAS may need permanent disability pensions that will enable them to work part-time or full-time in low-paying jobs and still live decently; most will need a trustee to ensure that bills get paid.

I learned that there was no cure or treatment for this disease, and it wouldn't dissipate with age, physical growth, or maturity; it's lifelong and irreversible. This confirmed what I had already experienced with Bobby: daily functioning would become more difficult to manage as he got older.

I felt redeemed; maybe it wasn't my fault. I felt vindicated. And then I felt guilty. Why hadn't I taken his learning disabilities seriously? Why hadn't I seen this before now? I knew at a young age that both of his biological parents were alcoholics. They drank with my grandmother whenever they were in town. My mother had told me about their drinking and that she thought Ronnie had dropped acid when she was pregnant with Bobby. After he was born, they would hang out in bars, drinking all day, while he slept in his seat. But this line of guilt-ridden thinking wasn't fair to my mother or me.

I wished I had read Dorris' book earlier. "Whether children are raised in the chaotic household of their unreformed alcoholic biological mothers or nurtured in stable, sober, loving natural or adoptive homes, the disabilities surface with uniformity."

I had never considered that there might be a reason for his behavior all those years. I was too consumed with pretending he didn't have any problems. That being rescued by my family was enough to make him normal, just like us. That if I could just *say* the right thing, he would *do* the right thing. If I could be a good enough sister, he could be the brother I needed him to be.

The more I learned about FAS over the next few months, the more empowered I felt. There was a name for it. There was a reason. Other people had been through the same thing with their children, and some with their brothers and sisters. I also learned that it was difficult to get a diagnosis. Most doctors didn't recognize it. When Bobby was born in 1975, fetal alcohol syndrome was still a new concept. Most people didn't know anything about it. The earliest recorded observation of potential links between maternal alcohol use and damage to the fetus was made in 1899. However, it wasn't until 1973—two years before Bobby was born—that fetal alcohol syndrome was specifically identified and named. More than thirty years later, it is still vastly misunderstood and unrecognized by most of the population. Also in the 1970s, the United States was just beginning the long process of shifting cultural norms in regard to all disabilities. In 1978, the National Council on Disability was established, and it wasn't until 1990 that the Americans with Disability Act became law. The work continues in our country to change old paradigms, especially in the definition and conceptualization of disability.

Getting Bobby diagnosed would be very difficult, especially thirty or so years after his birth. But I decided to try. I wanted him to have all the help available to him, the help he had always deserved. My research said that you needed to get school records, especially psychological evaluations, adoption records, that you should build a file with pictures and notes from his youth. And so I did.

I mailed letters to his elementary, middle, and high schools. I mailed a letter to the Department of Social Services requesting his adoption records. I started quizzing my mother for any details she could remember. I dug through boxes to find pictures from when he first came to live with us. My mother gave me the diary she had kept at that time. She also gave me letters she had written to Bobby's caseworker while he was still a foster child living with us. I received answers—answers to questions I didn't know I had. My eyes were opened to things I barely remembered, things I had heard before but never really knew.

I read the elementary school psychological case summary. Bobby had started kindergarten on schedule but was held back a year and still had significant difficulties in first grade. Since he was classified as severe speech/language impaired with average-to-low abilities, he was assigned speech therapy. By second grade, he was reclassified as learning disabled in reading, math, and writing.

"Overall growth from the 1983 evaluation can best be described as minimal," the middle school report read. At age eleven, his reading and spelling were at a second grade level. I wanted to scream at the teachers and the psychologists and my mother, "Why? Why didn't you *do* anything?" There's no mention in the reports of strategies or plans to address his deficiencies other than keeping the labeling in place.

I became angry with my mother. Why wasn't she more involved? Why hadn't she forced the school to help him? But, the more I thought about it, I realized that my mother didn't have experience with learning disabilities and at that time didn't know where to find resources or help. Her own parents had never valued education. My mother was the first in her family to graduate from high school, and no one from her family even attended her ceremony. She hadn't been overly involved with me or my brother and sisters because school came easy for us. So she hadn't known how to help Bobby.

I remembered when she saw a commercial for Sylvan Learning Center and signed him up. It was seventy-five dollars per session, which meant something had to be cut from the budget that week, and it was an hour drive from our home. She drove him there after school for as long as she could afford it. Bobby did better when he had one-on-one instruction, but he couldn't duplicate the work on his own, which frustrated him and my mother.

When I read in the middle school report, "mainstream children tend to make him angry," I asked Bobby about it. The school placed Bobby in mainstream classes whenever possible. Bobby hated being in the "special" class, but he hated his mainstream classes too. He was embarrassed, he said, because the other kids always knew he was from the "special" class, and the mainstream classes were full of preppy kids. To Bobby, the preppy kids were the ones who never did anything wrong, always got their homework done, and knew the answer when the teacher called on them. Kids he had nothing in common with. He especially hated lunchtime. His teacher would line up his class in the hallway and they would walk as a group to the cafeteria for lunch. This was when the preppy kids would yell, "Here come the retards" or "Hey, retard" as they passed by.

As I began to read the high school report, I realized nothing had changed from elementary or middle school. The report began with, "Bob has been evaluated three times previously and has consistently been found to be functioning cognitively within the low average to borderline range."

In spite of his challenges at school, Bobby was easy to get along with: "Bob seems to have established positive relationships with peers and most adults." He could talk to adults and kids his own age, including the kids who teased him. He tried out for the football team and made it, even though Murray and Buckman, leaders of the preppy kids, told him he'd never be able to do it. Sometimes he would play for a few minutes in the fourth quarter—if the team was winning. He loved to wear the jersey every Friday to school along with everyone else on the team.

"At this time, Bob is expected to successfully complete the requirements for a local high school diploma..." they had determined by the second paragraph of the same report. Really? The final paragraph concluded the report with statements such as, "If Bob would just organize himself better...if he would just do the work...he seems to be on track for a high school diploma...Bob has not developed the appropriate problem-solving skills that he needs to become a strong advocate for himself." The reports never mentioned what the school would do to help him. The consensus was that if Bobby would just work harder, study more, and become more organized, he could be like everyone else his age.

The final sentence of the middle school report read, "His slow rate of processing is an important factor." The term "intellectual disability" didn't exist in the early eighties. Bobby couldn't move as fast as the mainstream, yet his IQ was two points above the threshold for mental retardation. He was lost somewhere between labels.

I became determined to get the diagnosis he needed and to get him whatever help I could. I contacted The Arc, the Office of Vocational and Educational Services for Individuals with Disabilities (VESID) in New York, the Learning Disabilities Association of Central New York, the Office of Temporary and Disability Assistance, the Social Security Administration, and Medicaid.

I also applied for Bobby at the Office of Mental Retardation and Developmental Disabilities (OMRDD) in New York, which has since changed its name to the Office for People With Developmental Disabilities (OPWDD). Bobby was assigned a counselor named Shrity, a young woman who had recently earned her master's degree in philosophy. Part of the application process was for Shrity to perform an updated psychological evaluation of Bobby and a clinical interview with both of us. Shrity also reviewed his school reports and administered the Wechsler Individual Achievement Test in order to measure his intelligence.

After two days of testing and interviews, Bobby and I sat on one side of a conference table; Shrity sat opposite us and reviewed the results. The results were sobering, but after the last few months

I wasn't surprised. "Bobby's overall IQ is 72, the third percentile of his peers, which is in the borderline range of intellectual functioning." Border of what? Border of what society sees as mentally retarded and normal?

"My biggest concern for Robert," Shrity continued, "is that he scored a 66 in processing speed. He ranked in the first percentile." She put her paper down and looked at me as she said, "If the world would just slow down a little for Robert, he would do better." Borderline was a no-man's-land. It was the rut underneath the merry-go-round.

VESID also responded to my request. Their focus was on helping Bobby find a job consistent with his strengths and abilities, providing on-the-job coaching, and advocating with his employer to help him keep a job for longer than six months. This process began with a five-day skills assessment performed by an evaluator named Patricia at the Boards of Cooperative Educational Services (BOCES) in Liverpool, New York. A few weeks after Patricia completed the assessment, she asked Bobby and me to come in and discuss the results.

Bobby and I walked in the conference room. The room was empty except for the oblong conference table surrounded by at least twenty chairs. One wall, on the long side, was all windows with a view of the parking lot. The opposite wall was also one long window with a view of the hallway. Patricia and the counselor from VESID were already seated next to each other at the table. Bobby followed me to the opposite side, and we sat across from them with a view of the hallway. I looked at Patricia and the counselor expectantly, still hopeful that they had uncovered some hidden talent or mental ability that had gone untapped in Bobby.

Patricia stood up and closed the door.

"Robert, can you tell us what your dream job is?" she asked as she began the meeting.

I didn't want to answer for him, so I stayed silent and waited to hear Bobby's answer.

His face turned red as he shifted in his seat. "What I really want is to own my own store, you know, a convenience store." The other counselor, Patricia, and I all shifted uncomfortably in our seats.

"You definitely seem to like working with people," the counselor chimed. "We think food service might be a good option for you." *Dishwasher, I thought.* "Also, we thought you might like to work outdoors." *Cart pusher, janitor.*

Bobby and I were quiet as she explained further that they had found things he was more suited for and areas that could pique his interest.

"We are concerned that his work pace is not fast enough to meet any of the Department of Labor's scores," Patricia said. *Again, too slow.* She continued reviewing the education section and talked about his third grade reading level and his second grade math level.

"Robert is not a candidate for additional schooling or a GED," she said. "His abilities were too low, he was too slow." I tuned out her voice, unable to listen anymore. Heat rushed to my face and my stomach lurched uncomfortably. Patricia kept talking while I remembered every time in the last ten years that I had said to Bobby...*get your GED... you have to get your GED... you'll never earn more than minimum wage without your GED.* I encouraged him. I told him he could do it. I told him I believed in him. If he just applied himself, studied with a tutor, if he really wanted it, he could do it.

I was wrong.

I was no different than those school psychologists who expected him to graduate despite the evidence that he wouldn't. And in that conference room, when I heard Patricia say that he wasn't a candidate for a GED, I knew I had been wrong all along. I believed I had failed Bobby in the worst way.

I had always been defensive when friends, family, or strangers referred to my brother as slow. I hated that term. I thought it was a euphemism that was outdated and politically incorrect. But it turns out it's true. The first definition of the word slow in the *Merriam-Webster Dictionary* is "mentally dull, stupid." That is offensive. It doesn't seem to really capture his struggle. Bobby's brain was moving at a pace slower than 99 percent of his peers. I liked the third definition of slow better—"moving, flowing, or proceeding without rapidity or at less than the usual speed."

I discovered that the closest specialist to us who diagnosed patients with fetal alcohol syndrome was Luther K. Robinson, MD and Director of Dysmorphology and Clinical Genetics at Women & Children's Hospital of Buffalo. I called his office to make an appointment, and to my surprise, they could get us in right away, but Bobby didn't have insurance. We were waiting for a hearing to get his Medicaid reinstated, again. I scheduled the appointment for two months later, determined to keep it with or without insurance.

Five months after I first looked up FAS on the Internet at my mother's house, Bobby and I drove to Buffalo. My mother came with us. I think she came for Bobby but also because she was worried about me. That Tuesday morning happened to be just one week after I discovered that Kevin had been having an affair. The marriage I thought I had did not exist. I was devastated, Kevin was staying in a hotel, and I was undecided at that point if I was going to take him back or not. In the middle of Bobby's crisis I suddenly was having one of my own. But I had waited months for this appointment for Bobby, and there was no way I was going to miss it.

We sat in the waiting room at the hospital waiting to see Dr. Robinson. The clock ticked loudly; we jumped every time we heard a door close in the hall. We didn't know what to expect. The weight of the previous months' psychological testing, job skills evaluations, and interviews with countless government agencies filled the room with silent expectation. Finally, the nurse came to the door and called Bobby's name. We followed her down the hall to the examining room.

Bobby sat on the paper-covered table while I sat in a chair on the side. We were both quiet. I read a chart on the wall about epileptic seizures while we waited.

The doctor came in the examining room and shook my hand and Bobby's as he introduced himself. He took a comprehensive history. I had sent him Bobby's school reports, the psychological evaluation he had just completed, his adoption records, and childhood pictures ahead of time so that he could study them. He examined Bobby for more than an hour. At the end of the appointment, he sat in the chair directly across from Bobby, looked into his eyes, and told him he believed he suffered from the effects of alcohol-related neurodevelopmental disorder (ARND) within the spectrum of fetal alcohol spectrum disorder (FASD). I was relieved to have the confirmation but also incredibly sad for him as my throat knotted up and my eyes filled.

Bobby was quiet on the ride home from Buffalo, so was my mother. I believed she was sad too and probably disappointed that we hadn't had this information earlier in his life.

"What did you think of Dr. Robinson?" I asked. I looked at Bobby in the backseat through my rearview mirror.

"He was nice."

"What do you think about what he said? About you having fetal alcohol syndrome?"

He shrugged his shoulders.

"Good, I guess," he said. After a moment he added, "At least I'm not just a loser."

Less than a week later, we received Dr. Robinson's written report and diagnosis. He summarized his findings from the exam, noting Bobby's "short stature, truncal obesity, the suboptimal quality of his cognitive and adaptive skills... his prenatal exposures to alcohol, and postnatally his learning disabilities, academic under-achievement, under employment, and host of social problems..."

His report explained that "experience with individuals with FASD demonstrates that this congenital condition is chronic, long-standing, and interferes with adequate learning, occupational, and social functioning...long-term adult supervision likely will be needed..."

The diagnosis wouldn't change anything. It wouldn't change the fact that most people don't know what FAS is or why it matters. It wouldn't make Bobby's life any different. But it changed us. It changed me. It began to shift my thinking away from myself, my perspective, to Bobby's. It forced me to let go of the illusion that I had held onto since the day I first met him: that I could make everything okay. I couldn't. I couldn't fix him. I couldn't deny any longer that he was different, that he struggled to understand, that he wasn't like me or my brother and sisters, that he wasn't like 99 percent of people his own age. I began to see that it was never my responsibility or within my power to fix him, it was never my job to rescue him. The school psychologists, the adult psychologist, the VESID evaluator, and now Dr. Robinson all agreed that Bobby's behavior wasn't rebellious or purposeful in its hurt, or ignorant in its recurrence; it was simply a result of the way he is. The way he was born. Things happened to him in the womb that forever changed who he was and what he was capable of.

...numb

I WIPED MY NOSE WITH A TISSUE AND LOOKED AT Dr. Marsha. She was sitting still, waiting on me.

"I don't know what I'm feeling. Honestly. I feel numb. On Sunday, Kevin and I went for a walk and we talked a lot about my feelings, but I realized I don't really know what they are. I have trouble naming them. I cry a lot, but I don't know why." I was still crying there on her couch and reached for more tissues.

Dr. Marsha didn't say anything, but her gaze never left me. I had nothing else to say. She never looked away. Finally, she spoke. "Why do you think that is, Kelly?"

"I don't know. I think I do things to numb my feelings, like eat too much and drink too much."

I told Dr. Marsha that one thing I was aware of about myself is that I was an emotional eater and drinker. I turned to food for comfort when I was bored or lonely. I had probably lost the same twenty pounds at least five times in my adult life. I used pizza, nachos, and beer to soothe my feelings.

"Actually, Kelly, I don't think you're doing these things to numb your feelings. I think you're doing these things to avoid feeling them at all."

Dr. Marsha continued on with her theory that the only way to really soothe feelings was to first identify them. I wasn't soothing my feelings. I was trying not to acknowledge that they existed.

We talked about our very first session when I told her how panic punched me in the chest. A few hours after Kevin left our home the night I discovered his affair and went to stay at a hotel, my sister Shelly had called me.

"I'm worried about Kevin," Shelly said.

I was sitting at our dining room table when she called. I had been sifting through memories of how excited we were when we found this home. We had driven by this building for years, eyeing the private gardens on the rooftop, peering in the nine-foot windows, envying the people who lived inside, longing for a place there but never thinking it was possible. And then one day our realtor called us and asked us to look at a two-bedroom that was for sale.

We knew as soon as we walked in the door: the bright light from the big windows, the hardwood floors, the library ladder in the kitchen, and the blue porcelain master bath. We fell in love with it immediately. This was the home we'd been looking for. This was our dream home.

"Why? What's he doing? You talked to him?" I asked her.

"He called me. I think he's drunk. Said he drank a lot of wine."

"I bet he has. He should be drinking. He fucked up," I said.

"He told me he had taken some pills too," Shelly said.

"What?" I stood up and began pacing. I knew he had a large supply of clonazepam that he kept on hand for his panic attacks.

"He's slurring his words. He's really messed up."

I hung up with my sister and called Kevin's cell. I stayed on the phone long enough to get his room number, and then I called my dad. I convinced him to come with me to the hotel and take Kevin to the emergency room. It didn't matter that it was ten o'clock at night or that my own life was shattered. I should have been the one drunk and taking too many pills, wallowing in my own grief, but instead I spent the next five hours into the early morning of the next day making sure that Kevin, the man who had betrayed me, was going to be okay.

Dr. Marsha helped me see that I turned to Kevin and his problems because it allowed me to avoid myself. It allowed me to sidestep my own anger, devastation, sadness, and grief. I worried about everyone else not only to keep the peace and make them happy but to avoid my own feelings. I had become such a master at diverting my attention that I had become numb, like I didn't even have feelings anymore. I realized that the peace I was always striving to keep was the peace I got by avoiding what was really upsetting me and by evading what was really disturbing *my* peace.

I had created a pattern of constantly moving and of focusing on other people, including Bobby, because I didn't want to admit that I needed something. That's what I did. I kept moving. I kept fixing. If I stood still, then I would feel my own pain; that was something I had spent a lifetime trying not to do.

SEIZED BY NUMBNESS

NARCOLEPSY SNUCK INTO BOBBY'S LIFE WHEN WE weren't looking; in fact, we barely noticed at first. It started when Bobby was twenty-six or so, living at the leaning house on Walnut Street and working at the casino. When he first told me about his legs giving out at work, causing him to fall to the ground, his tray of drinks spilling on his uniform, and his glasses breaking as they hit the floor, I didn't think too much of it. And then it happened again. And then I witnessed it. I was with Bobby in my mother's kitchen and we were laughing. I don't remember what was so funny, but Bobby was laughing pretty hard. His legs crumpled suddenly, and he fell with all his weight against the dryer. That's when I knew something was happening in his body. When I began to research the symptom of one's legs losing strength, I had no idea where to start. I typed the expression "legs give out when laughing" in the search window and discovered a name for what Bobby had been experiencing: cataplexy. I kept reading and learned that cataplexy is often a symptom of narcolepsy.

Narcolepsy is a chronic neurological disorder caused by the brain's inability to regulate sleep-wake cycles, resulting in the overwhelming urge to sleep. Excessive daytime sleepiness (EDS) is the major symptom that characterizes narcolepsy.

Anytime Bobby was still for more than a minute or two, he fell asleep. When Bobby got in my car, he fell asleep before I turned the corner. I wouldn't let him have a drink in my car after a cup of coffee dropped out of his hand when he dozed off and spilled all over the carpet and seat. He fell asleep while eating at the dinner table, his face landing in his plate of food. He fell asleep in the middle of a conversation. He even fell asleep while sitting on the toilet.

Cataplexy is the most common major symptom of narcolepsy other than EDS, occurring in about 70 percent of narcolepsy patients. The person can experience sudden loss of muscle tone leading to feelings of weakness and a loss of voluntary muscle control, which means that Bobby can be standing still or walking or sitting in a chair and then suddenly fall over. All 225 pounds of him can suddenly become lifeless, and he is unable to move until his legs regain their strength. He doesn't lose consciousness during these episodes, but he can't speak and he can't stop it once it starts. He has to wait it out. Cataplexy can occur spontaneously and can be triggered by sudden, strong emotions such as fear, anger, stress, excitement, or laughter. It seems to happen often when Bobby least expects it. After dinner one night, he was putting his pan of leftover shepherd's pie in the refrigerator. The pan was still warm with his favorite comfort food—mashed potatoes, peas, beef, and gravy—that our Mom used to make for us when we were young. As Bobby bent over to find room on the middle shelf, he fell hard into the metal microwave rack next to his refrigerator and gouged a wound in his side and stomach. When I saw him a few days later, there was a deep, purple gash from his chest to his waist.

As I learned more about narcolepsy, I passed the information on to the rest of my family. Some of the things we had been noticing in Bobby began to make sense. Several people, including my mother, often thought Bobby was drunk or stoned because his eyes were droopy and his speech slurred. He wasn't, this was just what he looked and acted like with EDS. He wasn't falling asleep all the time because he was lazy. It wasn't because he was overweight; in fact, obesity can be a side effect of narcolepsy.

Because of his symptoms, Bobby became self-conscious in front of strangers and people he didn't know well. One Sunday afternoon at my niece's birthday party, my sisters, my mother, and I were all on high alert. While we sat in the shade and watched the kids play in the pool, we also kept a close eye on Bobby and remained alert for specific signs that cataplexy was imminent. His body would sway back and forth, his steps would weave right and left, his eyes would close, and then we knew he was about to go down. When it was time to eat that day, he walked back to the table with a plate piled high with chicken, potatoes, corn, and salad in one hand and a drink in the other. He paused for a moment about halfway there and started to sway. Before any of us could get to him, he lost his balance, fell to his knees, and dropped his plate of food. My sisters and I jumped up to help. We picked up his food and got him a new plate. The in-laws and other guests stared and whispered for a minute or two before going back to their conversations.

Narcolepsy may have snuck in, but it was here to stay and demanded that we take notice. I explained narcolepsy to Bobby and shared all that I had learned. Bobby tried talking to his family doctor about his symptoms, but the doctor wouldn't listen. This wasn't unusual. Receptionists, doctors, and nurses didn't really *see* him. They usually didn't have the patience to wait while Bobby got his words out. He was easily intimidated and often didn't understand what they said to him; they didn't take the time to explain.

For his next appointment, I sent Bobby with information I had printed from the Internet about narcolepsy. The physician's assistant read the information and researched it herself. She prescribed Provigil for Bobby, a controlled substance, which is a stimulant used to treat EDS.

It was a major accomplishment to have something that would help him stay awake; however, it was very expensive. Bobby had been stuck in an endless loop of insurance issues. If he had a job, he would lose any Medicaid benefits because he "makes too much money." Then he couldn't afford the Provigil. Without Provigil he couldn't stay awake long enough to get through his shift and he would lose his job. Once he lost his job, he would apply for and get Medicaid reinstated, only to lose it again when he got a new job.

I began to notice the discrimination against people with intellectual disabilities. Our culture values strength over weakness, intellect over character, and accomplishment over a simpler life. Therefore, a segment of our population is systemically and repeatedly marginalized—unseen and unheard. When someone has physical disabilities that are invisible and intellectual limitations that aren't always obvious, life is challenging in ways that most of us don't understand.

You wouldn't know any of this about my brother when you first looked at him. He looks like any other thirty-something guy. We need to allow for the possibility that we can't see everything at first glance. Most people have a reason why they can't do what we expect them to do. There is a reason why they can't move as fast as the rest of us, why they stand when they're supposed to be sitting, why they fall asleep when they should be awake, why they hold a sign on a street corner when we think they should be working.

A supervisor with the Onondaga County Department of Social Services once told me, "Robert will get no help from this agency. It is his responsibility to get the help he needs." The last time his benefits were discontinued because he made too much at his seven-dollar-an-hour job, he didn't realize he had a right to a fair hearing. Nobody told him this verbally. By the time I read the packet of papers that had been mailed to him with notice of his discontinuation of benefits, the deadline to request a fair hearing had passed and his benefits had already been cancelled.

I contacted the company that manufactures Provigil, completed a ten-page application for assistance, and attached his most recent tax return showing just how little money he made. I was thrilled when Bobby received six vouchers for the medicine. These vouchers bought me six months to figure out how to get him on Medicaid permanently. I applied for an emergency hearing on Bobby's behalf to explain why he needed to be on Medicaid. I was sure that once they heard about his medical problems and the fact that he wanted to work but couldn't without his medicine, logic would prevail and his application would be approved.

On Tuesday, April 3, 2007, I attended a fair hearing for Bobby to get his Medicaid benefits reinstated on the basis of his inability to work without his medical treatment, arguing that the wages they based his ineligibility on were not sustainable. It was my opportunity to tell an administrative law judge why I thought the decision about Bobby's case was wrong. Then the Office of Temporary and Disability Assistance would provide me with a written decision that stated whether the local agency's decision was right or wrong, potentially ordering the local agency to correct our case.

The hearing did not go well. When I explained his learning disabilities along with the physical issues, they directed me to one of their agencies' programs: Medicaid for people with disabilities. After the hearing, I stopped at the Medicaid office to get more information. The gentleman at the counter went to look for the only person in the office who knew anything about the program. She was out to lunch. He came back with a fifteen-part form accompanied by a twenty-page instruction booklet. How is someone who reads at a third grade level supposed to navigate this? If someone in a wheelchair came in and was told the only way to get help was to climb a set of stairs, the agency would be hit with a lawsuit. Why was it okay to discriminate against people with invisible disabilities?

While I waited for a decision from the Medicaid hearing, Bobby became ill. I spoke to him one Sunday night on the phone. He told me he didn't feel well and was having trouble breathing. His voice was weak, his words muffled with a wheezing sound. After I hung up, I couldn't stop thinking about him. I decided it was better to risk overreacting, so Kevin and I drove to his apartment. We walked in his living room and found him sitting in his chair, pale, weak, unable to get up. His breathing was heavy; he could barely speak. I called 911 and rode with him in the ambulance to the emergency room. He spent a week in the hospital with pneumonia. He lost his job at Denny's, but the social worker at the hospital helped us get his Medicaid reinstated.

Now that he had insurance, I made an appointment for him at the neurology clinic at Upstate University Hospital. This was the first time he was examined by a neurologist. Frustrated that doctors didn't seem to take Bobby seriously, I had decided that I would not only go to every doctor's appointment with him but I would also go in the examining room. I explained to the doctor why I was convinced he had narcolepsy. I told him about the cataplexy, and the EDS that had started about six years ago, and how the incidents happened more and more often now. I explained that the physician's assistant at his primary care doctor had prescribed Provigil, and it seemed to help. I asked the neurologist about other treatments for narcolepsy, specifically cataplexy. Despite my research, medical conclusions, and stories of Bobby's daily life, the doctor refused to treat him for narcolepsy without an official diagnosis. I refused to leave the examining room until he agreed to refer Bobby for a multiple sleep latency test—the test used to diagnose narcolepsy.

A couple of weeks after the appointment, the sleep lab received his referral. I called to make the appointment and was told they were scheduling into next year for "Medicaid patients." I told the woman scheduling the appointment that that was unacceptable. She referred me to another sleep lab—they were scheduling six months out. I called their office every day for a week and begged for a closer appointment. They finally agreed to put us on the cancellation list, and a couple of weeks later we got on the schedule for the test.

Three months after the first appointment with the neurologist, Bobby and I sat in the sleep lab waiting room. He had been scheduled for this test once before, about three years ago. A few minutes in, they discovered he had sleep apnea and cancelled the rest of the test. Therefore, there was no narcolepsy diagnosis. They couldn't assess whether or not he had narcolepsy until they treated the sleep apnea and were confident he had received a sound night's sleep before the test. The medical reasoning for this may be logical; however, it seemed senseless and frustrating to me and had needlessly delayed a proper diagnosis.

The waiting room at the sleep clinic, a small square room lined with vinyl chairs, was empty. The receptionist nodded to us from behind the sliding glass window and said she'd be right with us. It was 9:00 p.m., and we were tired, quiet, and both of us nervous for different reasons. I knew how important this test was. I knew we had to have an official diagnosis to get the neurologist to treat Bobby, and I knew we needed it to get some financial assistance in addition to his Medicaid. Bobby was nervous at the thought of having to spend the night with strangers while tubes and wires anchored him to machines. I told him I wasn't going to stay all night, but I wouldn't leave until he was settled and I would be back in the morning to pick him up.

The receptionist slid the glass open and called out, "Robert Bargabos." She gave him a clipboard with papers. He handed them to me and I filled them out. I turned the forms in and we waited in the quiet room. The door opened and two orderlies, dressed in white shirts and white pants, waited at the door. They were ready for Bobby and would escort him to the testing area. I stood in the doorway and watched as they led him away. Walking down the hallway, he started to weave back and forth, and before I could shout out a warning that he was ready to go down, his legs gave out and he crashed into the orderlies, knocking them into the wall before he landed on the floor. The orderlies yelled out for help as they struggled to get him up. Two nurses came running with panic on their faces. I explained that they had just witnessed his cataplexy, assured them he would be okay in a few minutes, and that this was just something that happened.

This time they performed the full test. I was anxious for the official report, and after a few days, I called the sleep lab and spoke with the attending physician. He told me "Robert is a classic textbook case of narcolepsy." He mentioned the cataplectic episode in the waiting room and that he observed Bobby falling asleep later that night while getting water, during lunch the next day, and during conversation. The doctor assured me the written report would reflect this diagnosis. A week later we had the official report and diagnosis.

This was the second diagnosis in three months for Bobby. Just like FAS, this was a diagnosis of a disease for which there is no cure. A diagnosis that explains the symptoms that had seized Bobby's body and his life but won't change what is happening.

The word narcolepsy comes from two Greek words roughly translated as "seized by numbness." Experts don't know for sure what causes it. Studies have shown that the neurological disorder may be caused by a number of genetic or biological factors in the brain, combined with an environmental trigger during the brain's development, such as a virus. I couldn't help but wonder if it was related to his FAS diagnosis, and that the environmental trigger in his case could be the alcohol and drugs his mother consumed while she was pregnant with him, or maybe it was the malnutrition he suffered as a baby, or the trauma resulting from his infant head hitting a wall.

At the same time we were working on the narcolepsy diagnosis, the VESID program began to assist Bobby in looking for a job. They helped him apply and get the interview. They also explained to the employer some of Bobby's challenges to ensure he received a fair shot at the job. I was excited to have someone else advocate for Bobby. With their help, he applied at a local car dealership for a maintenance position. The job actually paid a little more than minimum wage and was on the bus line. It sounded perfect for him. It was also his birthday, so Kevin and I planned to take him to dinner to celebrate. One of his favorite things was to go out to eat. We picked him up at his apartment, and while we drove to the restaurant he'd selected, I asked him what was happening with the job interview.

"I didn't get the job."

"I thought you had the job."

"They called me today and told me I didn't get it."

"I don't understand. They had a job opening, you applied. The guy from VESID said it was a done deal. What happened?"

"I dunno."

"Well, what did they say?"

"They said I failed the drug test."

"What? " I whipped around in my seat to look at him, luckily Kevin was driving. "What do you mean you failed the drug test? How is that possible?"

"I dunno." He shrugged his shoulders and stared out the window. He wouldn't look at me.

"Bob! How did you fail the drug test?"

"I smoked some pot the other night."

I pounded the back of my seat. "Why would you do that? Since when do you smoke pot?" I knew my voice was too loud and high pitched in the small car.

"I don't."

"But you did the other night? With who?"

"Dave."

"Dave who?"

"The building super."

"You smoked pot with the building super. That's great. That's just fucking great. I can't believe you did that. All the work I've done to get you hooked up with VESID; how am I going to explain this? You're going to get kicked out of the program. They're not going to help you if you fail drug tests."

Bobby stared out the window. He still wouldn't look at me. Yelling at Bobby never really worked well. He would clam up and stop speaking.

"Say something. How much pot are you smoking?"

"I don't. I just did it the other night because I thought it would help me sleep. I can't fall asleep at night after taking my medicine all day to keep me up."

"That's it? That's your reason?" He stopped talking, and I didn't want to yell anymore. I turned back around in my seat and stared out the window. By this time, we had arrived at the restaurant. Neither Bobby nor I said a word as we got out of the car, walked inside, and were led to a table. Bobby and I sat across from each other with Kevin between us. We avoided each other's eyes while my anger hung over the table. After all we'd been through in the last nine months together—the FAS diagnosis, the narcolepsy diagnosis, the doctor's appointments, the forms, the struggle to get his Medicaid and medicine—I felt like this was a setback. The menus arrived in silence.

"So, what's everybody getting?" Kevin asked.

"Chicken," I said.

"Spaghetti," Bob said.

The bread and salads arrived.

The spaghetti and chicken arrived.

Kevin looked at us, hoping one or the other would give in and start talking, but neither one did. No one ordered dessert. We ate our food and left. I had Kevin take me home first before he drove Bobby home.

After they dropped me off, I paced around my living room. I felt bad about my reaction when Bobby told me he failed the drug test.

The more I paced and the more I thought, the angrier I became. My anger turned away from Bobby and toward FAS and narcolepsy. I was angry they had taken Bobby's life hostage. I regretted that Bobby's birthday dinner had been ruined. I knew he hated it when I was mad at him. And it was a setback, for me, not him. I didn't want our relationship to be one in which he was always seeking my approval, and I was always mad at him for the reckless things he did without thinking them through. I knew better now. I knew that would never change. If one of us were hit by a bus tomorrow, I didn't want our last conversation to consist of me yelling and him feeling bad. I didn't have it all figured out yet, but I knew that wasn't love. And what if he was right? I didn't know what it was like to have narcolepsy. Smoking a little weed probably did make him feel better. Hell, with all of the shit going on in his life, maybe he *should* be smoking pot.

...fear

I SAT IN THE WAITING ROOM, INHALING THROUGH MY nose, exhaling through my mouth, meditating on the soft jazz notes soothing my nerves one at a time. It was stressful for me every time I had a one-on-one appointment with Dr. Marsha. *Should I go? Should I spend the money? Do I have anything to talk about?*

Her door opened and her voice snapped me out of my thoughts.

"Kelly. Are you ready? Come on in," she said.

Dr. Marsha had been pressing me to really consider my family of origin and my earliest memories: my mom's depression, my dad's alcoholism almost killing him, my mom threatening to leave him and us.

"I remember those things. But I don't remember how I felt at the time." I was frustrated. She was being pushy. I thought we were done talking about those early childhood memories.

"Imagine it. You're six years old and you're begging your mother not to leave you. Or you're seven years old and you visit your dad in the hospital to say goodbye forever. How would that make you feel today?" She was not letting up.

"I'm sure I would be scared most of all. Sad. Nervous. Afraid."

"What do you feel in your body right now when you think of this happening? Or when someone you love is going through something awful?"

"I feel uneasy and anxious, a pit in my stomach, my chest gets so tight it hurts to breathe."

"Exactly. You feel fear," Dr. Marsha said.

We spent the rest of our time together talking about fear and how this insidious weed took root in my mind and soul as a child and had directed my decisions and behavior ever since—the fear of my family splitting up, fear of having children, fear of ending up like my mother, fear of alcoholism, fear of conflict, fear of wrong decisions, fear of not having enough money, fear of losing Bobby, fear of losing my home.

She reminded me of the time I told her that I was always worried and afraid that our house wasn't neat enough and would take it upon myself to vacuum and clean so I wouldn't be embarrassed. *Where did this come from? Why was I so afraid for people to see that I'm less than perfect?*

I struggled to accept her theory. It was hard for me to believe I was driven by fear. Most people who knew me would say I was fearless. They would say I was smart and independent and brave. I had overcome fear in many situations. I did my first triathlon at forty-two years old and learned to swim in open waters through all panic and doubt, bike for miles, and finish with a run. I never thought I could do that, yet I did. I read my own essays and poems in front of strangers and loved it. I presented financial reports and business plans to the CEO and the board of directors. I had courage.

After our appointment was over, Dr. Marsha's words still nagged at me. I took out my journal and began to write my thoughts—without editing them.

I started with my father. I knew he loved me. I've always known it. I've never doubted it. But in the deepest part of me, I wondered. Would he still love me if I quit my job to become a writer? Would he still love me if I divorced my husband? Would he still love me if he knew I was angry and not always happy? I believed God loved me unconditionally, but I constantly worried that I disappointed Him. I was afraid of becoming an alcoholic yet was as comfortable on a bar stool as I was in church. I was afraid that I would lose my brother.

I earned a six-figure salary, yet I worried about money all the time. I was afraid of never being what I was supposed to be. I was afraid I would never lose those twenty pounds permanently. I was still afraid of not being good enough, smart enough, or pretty enough.

I could eat in a restaurant alone, go to the movies by myself, sit alone at a bar, travel around the world solo, and yet, I was afraid to be myself with people because if they really knew me they wouldn't like me. I feared that without children, once my parents died, I would no longer exist.

Maybe Dr. Marsha was right.

HELP

BOBBY NEVER DID DEVELOP A POT-SMOKING HABIT or get mired in alcohol, which is amazing when I think about how alcoholism has coursed through my family's veins, hidden among the red-and-white blood cells and platelets. It hit every generation more than once, looking for the one to dominate and destroy—my grandmother, her brother, and their father before them; my father, his brother, their grandfather; my mother's sister, her brother, George; and of course, Ronnie. It was yet to be determined in my generation who among us would win or lose. But this was not one of Bobby's battles. For that I was grateful.

The VESID counselor took some convincing, but he eventually believed me that the failed drug test was an isolated incident and agreed to keep Bobby in the program. If he failed another test, they would send him for a full drug evaluation. Thankfully, that never happened. His job coach helped him get another position working as a dishwasher at the Greek bakery right up the street from his apartment. This meant he could walk from home, which was important since Bobby wasn't driving anymore. After his last car was stolen and totaled, I didn't make any effort to replace it, nor did my father.

Sleepiness was unavoidable, even with his medication, and we were afraid he would fall asleep again while driving and eventually kill himself or someone else. Bobby had to give up the freedom that came with driving himself to work, to the grocery store, and to his doctor's appointments. I lost that freedom as well, along with Kevin and my parents since we were responsible for driving him around.

Bobby had lived in the same place for more than a year now, ever since he left the John Milton Inn. He finally had a two-bedroom apartment and was very happy to have an actual dining room table, instead of one shoved in the corner of the kitchen, and more importantly, he had a second bedroom. He didn't have to sleep on the couch anymore when his daughter visited; she had her own room. He bought a purple comforter for her hand-me-down bed, and I gave her an old desk that I had painted soft blue with purple and pink flowers. It was the nicest apartment he'd had in a very long time. His landlord called me if there were any problems so I could stay one step ahead of any issues that might cause him to lose his home.

It didn't take long for the owner of the bakery to lose patience with Bobby's sleepiness. Bobby would stand over that day's baking pans, scrubbing them clean of the baked-on piecrust and donut residue, rinsing them with hot water, leaning up against the edge of the stainless steel sink. He would start out his shift determined to stay awake, stay alert, work hard, and make his boss proud; but with any pause in action—anytime he stood in one place for more than a few seconds—his eyes closed halfway, his movements became trance like. His hands still scrubbed, but the circles he made were slower and slower, smaller and smaller with each minute that passed. His arm reached out to turn on the faucet but didn't have quite enough will to reach it. His hand missed the nozzle again and again until his arm fell to his side, and his body became somewhat still, trapped in an unsolicited nap. A pan would fall to the floor, or his boss would yell, or the owner's son would hit him when he walked by, waking him up, and he'd start in on the same pan again. He couldn't go home until the pans were clean for the next day's baking, even if it took him twice as long on some nights to finish.

Bobby's job coach called me.

"The owner is disenchanted with Bob," he told me.

"Why's that?"

"He complained that Bobby was drowsy and seemed to work in slow motion. He had to send him home twice before he finished the pans. Doesn't want to pay overtime."

"He does know Bobby has narcolepsy, right?"

Of course he was drowsy and worked in slow motion. I thought having a job coach to intervene with the boss would help keep Bobby employed longer, but that wasn't working out like I'd hoped. Bobby liked to work, he wanted to work, and he needed the money. Even with his job, he didn't make enough to live on his own. I supplemented his income and made sure his bills were paid. Kevin never complained that Bobby's bills became budget items of ours; he took it more in stride than I did, even after he found himself unemployed. Probably because I had this thing about financial security—I needed it. I was good at managing my money but was slowly learning that it was impossible to control how other people spent their money. I couldn't sleep at night if my bank account was unreconciled. I also lost sleep worrying about whether my older brother would be able to find another job or pay his mortgage; I worried that my parents hadn't saved enough to retire. My therapist thought this was a problem.

A good therapist has a way of rearranging the pieces of your life so that a new picture comes into focus. You may have thought you had them fitted together nicely in a pattern that made sense. Then something happens that causes the puzzle that is your life to be upended, scattering the pieces on the floor, and you are faced with the task of finding the straight edges, the corners that anchor the scene, the innies and the outties, the similar colors and patterns that match, and piecing them all back together again. Kevin and I began seeing Dr. Marsha when we were upended by his affair. We were trying to figure out if our marriage could be picked up off the floor and put back together. We weren't ready to give up on us yet. I hadn't realized how much of our life's picture was set at a very young age. It didn't take too many sessions for her to figure me out. It all made sense to her, and it began to make sense to me.

"Of course you became an accountant," Dr. Marsha had exclaimed once, more animated than usual in one of my solo sessions with her. "One of your number one fears has been dependence on another person so that you wouldn't get trapped like your mother."

I was stunned. I did well in school. I was good at math. I even considered a math major but thought that wasn't interesting enough so I chose accounting. It was a very logical decision. At least that is how I remembered it. According to Dr. Marsha, accounting chose me.

There in her office, a new picture developed. As the pieces clicked into place, I saw that my mother had wanted to leave a bad relationship but was unable to because she had no money of her own and no skills to support herself. It made sense that I became an accountant. If I could manage money, I would never be dependent on anyone.

I promised Dr. Marsha that I would release the people I loved to live their own lives, make their own mistakes, and live out the consequences of their choices. Everyone that is, except Bobby. It was too late for us. He was hardwired in my psyche—we were soul mates.

But after crunching the numbers, I knew I couldn't financially support him forever. I kept thinking about what I had learned in *Damaged Angels*: the adult with FAS may need permanent disability pensions that will enable them to work part-time or full-time in low-paying jobs and still live decently; most will need a trustee to ensure that bills get paid. Bobby needed help. We needed help.

I scoured the Internet for agencies and phone numbers. I fit phone calls in between conference calls and employee issues at work. I did as much as I could over the phone, taking vacation time only when I had to take Bobby to an appointment or evaluation. I carried Bobby's life with me in an expanding file folder with slots labeled: Doctors, VESID, Medicaid, HUD, and Landlord. I could fax reports, diagnoses, copies of applications, and pay stubs at a moment's notice.

I would tell anybody who would listen, "I'm calling about my brother. He has fetal alcohol syndrome with a low IQ and learning disabilities. He also has narcolepsy." I learned after the first or second phone call that you had to skip politically correct lingo and go right to the honest and specific facts. "His IQ is 72. He reads at a second grade level, he's slow...." Terms like developmental disability or intellectually disabled were too broad, too abstract, not real enough. It was fine for the general public and worked at keeping labels from becoming slurs or names called for sport, but it just wasn't helpful when you were trying to paint the picture of my brother's life. With each phone call, I learned a little more about which agencies might be able to help him. People were very sympathetic but didn't sugarcoat how hard it would be to get help, especially when the disabilities weren't obvious. They gave me tips like, "When you fill out the application, make it sound like he'll be lucky to live another day."

I looked for help at the Central New York Developmental Services Offices (CNYDSO) for an eligibility determination with the OMRDD. Bobby was two IQ points above mental retardation, so he wouldn't qualify under that criteria. But he could still qualify for services if he met three major requirements for a developmental disability: a qualifying diagnosis, substantial impairment of daily functioning expected to last indefinitely, and existence of the disability prior to age twenty-two. I thought it was a slam dunk. We had the diagnosis, to me there was no doubt about his impairment of daily functioning, and by definition, FAS happened in the womb and therefore had to exist prior to age twenty-two even if it hadn't been diagnosed properly by then.

I completed the eleven-page application, filling out the financial section with mostly zeroes, and tried to fit Bobby's family history and his school and medical information within the lines of the form. I attached extra pages to describe how narcolepsy made everything harder and that I had to help him with this form because of his intellectual limitations. I wrote a cover letter explaining why Bobby needed their help and mailed the application in. I called the intake office a week later to make sure they received it. They requested more information. I faxed school reports and a copy of his Provigil prescription. A few weeks later, Wendy, the case manager called and told me that the CNYDSO did not agree with me, and his initial application was denied. I bombarded her with questions. What was the review process? Were you on the committee? Can I speak to someone who made the decision? Can Bobby get back on the agenda for the next meeting? What was the reason for the denial? Why doesn't he meet the criteria? Where can I get a written explanation of his rights? Are you following the process mandated by the state of New York?

Wendy patiently answered my questions and agreed to take Bobby's application through a second review process. Three weeks later, he was on the committee's agenda again. I called to see if I could attend the meeting; I thought that if I could explain his life to this committee, they couldn't help but approve him. They wouldn't let me attend the meeting. Wendy called me the day after the review.

"I'm sorry, Kelly. We had a really long discussion about your brother, but Robert's eligibility has been denied. He's not eligible for services based on a developmental disability."

"I don't understand. FAS by definition meets all three criteria," I argued. "Can you put him on the agenda again?"

"No, not unless there's new information to present. There is one more thing we can do—it's called a third step review," Wendy said.

Bobby's records were sent to Albany and reviewed by a panel of clinicians. I wrote a two-page letter with my arguments and assertions to add to his file before it was sent. Another two months went by before Wendy called me.

"The clinicians in Albany came to the same conclusion as the committee in Syracuse: he's been denied. They really struggled with the criteria that the disability existed prior to age twenty-two."

"But, it happened in the womb. Why don't they get that?"

"I'm really sorry, Kelly, but they were stuck on the reports from Bobby's school. They didn't feel like they supported a substantial impairment that would affect his daily functioning."

It was final. There would be no more reviews or hearings. Bobby would not find help here.

I moved on. My days were spent writing letters, filling out forms, making more phone calls, wondering if I'd get a call that Bobby had fallen and cracked his head open, worrying about my bank account, and how long my husband would be out of a job. At the same time,

I was angry. I was angry for Bobby but also for all the other people like Bobby. How did they manage? How did they fill out these forms if they couldn't read well? How did they get themselves to appointments if they couldn't drive? Is this why more than half a million people in our country end up homeless and living on our streets? There are many excellent programs in our society, safety nets that we are fortunate to have, programs that do not exist in most parts of our world. But, they are entangled in so much paperwork, committee reviews, and subjective opinions that the people who need them most can't access them. I wondered if many people just gave up.

Also, Bobby's cataplexy seemed to be happening more frequently. Sometimes he could feel it coming, and sometimes there was no warning. First, his knees buckled and his jelly-like legs went soft and limp. Then a wave of numbness moved through his brain until he couldn't make his mouth move, his voice was muted, his tongue unable to get out even simple words he wanted to say, words like "help." The numbness rolled through his arms and legs, pinning him on the living room or dining room floor, the pavement of a parking lot, or the floor in Walmart. They happened when he was home alone, when he was with strangers, and when he was with people he knew. It really didn't matter; nothing could be done. You had to stand by him and wait. Wait for its grip to loosen his body and tongue so you could help him up and see if he was hurt from the impact of the fall. These episodes were terrifying for Bobby and frightening for whoever was around. Strangers and neighbors wanted to call an ambulance. To those of us who knew him well, they seemed like seizures; even though that's not the medical term, that's what we called them. I kept a notepad by the phone:

5/26   *Picnic at Mom's. 1 seizure.*

5/30   *Left for vacation. 4 seizures that day, 2 in Mom &
        Dad's car.*

6/13   *7:00 a.m.— sitting in chair at table—fell out of it.*

6/19   *3 seizures—one at dining room table, woke up on
        the floor.*

6/27   *3 seizures.*

7/1   *Tuesday night—3 seizures @ dinner with Shelly.
        Had 7 or 8 throughout the day.*

7/8   *Seizure while riding his bike on South Bay Road.
        Fell into ditch and hit his head.*

7/10   *2 seizures at Walmart with his ex-wife and daughter.*

I was afraid for him. I tried not to think about the terrible things that could happen if he fell asleep or had cataplexy at the wrong time. I felt like time was running out. With every phone call, every seizure, every job lost, I worried he would never find help. Financial assistance wouldn't alleviate the medical issues, but I had to keep trying. Bobby wasn't "bad enough" to get help for his developmental disabilities, but his narcolepsy was proving to be debilitating so disability assistance through the Social Security Administration (SSA) seemed to be a possible solution.

Not only did I answer every question of that seventeen-page application, I attached definitions of narcolepsy and FAS, and I attached doctors' notes. I explained that Bobby wanted to be independent and productive in our society but needed a tremendous amount of support and understanding to cope with everyday life. How could they deny him? Again, I thought it was a slam dunk.

Weeks went by without any news, so I called the SSA office. I answered more questions, faxed in copies of recent medical and psych evaluations, and took Bobby to their doctors for examination. Several months had gone by when I finally received the determination letter in March 2008.

We have determined that your condition is not severe enough to keep you from working. You said you were disabled because of a breathing problem, high blood pressure, a condition which affects several parts of your body, a neurological problem, seizures, an emotional problem, alcoholism, obesity, sleepiness, a birth defect, learning problems, and a behavior problem. The medical evidence shows that you have had some shortness of breath, near normal examination findings, a weight problem, some difficulty in stressful situations, and a sleep problem. The reports did not show any other conditions of a nature that would prevent you from working.

Denied. They'd completely missed it. Breathing problem? Emotional problem? Alcoholism? I was incredulous at the malpractice that seemed so obvious to me. Anger and determination superseded my feelings of helplessness and frustration. I wouldn't let myself cry or give up. I knew I was right; I had the facts on my side. I had to believe the facts would win over inept management of these programs that were designed to help people like my brother. I realized I had been naïve to think that the facts would be enough. I finally had to admit I needed help.

My sister, Shelly, an attorney, connected me with a law firm that specialized in disability claims; they started the appeal process on Bobby's behalf. I discovered there is an entire legal industry to help people file disability claims. I was relieved to know that someone else was helping me fight this battle, even though they would take one-third of his claim as their fee. I never felt like the lawyer was moving fast enough. Bobby's disability claim was one of many. He was just another client who no one within the law firm had even met. I still called the agency office directly, which frustrated the paralegal at the attorney's office, and prompted a phone call to my sister. I learned that I could request a hearing as soon as possible, based on financial hardship. I wrote another letter to the SSA.

> I would like to request a hearing as soon as possible based on financial hardship. Robert has tried for many years to support himself, but because of his narcolepsy, FAS, intellectual disabilities, and the resulting limitations, he just does not have the ability to do that. He is unable to pay his rent or utilities. I have been paying his rent and utility bill in order to keep a roof over his head and to keep him off the street. My brother has been homeless in the past, and I am trying to prevent this from happening again. My contribution averages $700 per month. I am attaching copies of checks written for rent and utilities. This is placing a financial strain on me and my family, and I'm unable to continue this for eighteen months while we wait for a hearing. Can we schedule a hearing as soon as possible?

Bobby was just as devastated with the latest denial as I was, and just as exhausted. His body and mind had been poked and prodded by psychologists, caseworkers, nurses, and doctors for more than a year now. He sat silently next to me at every evaluation, every conference, every doctor's appointment and listened while I explained what he was like, and what life was like for him, pleading for somebody to *see* him. He never questioned what I was doing; he trusted me. I kept telling him that help was out there for him, and we would find it together. He believed me. One afternoon, Bobby called me with an idea.

"Hey, what do you think about calling Hillary?"

"Hillary who?"

"You know, Senator Clinton. I see her on TV. She's from New York, and she seems like she sticks up for people like me."

"I don't know if she gets involved in this stuff, Bob." I was doubtful. Not because I doubted Hillary's abilities or compassion, but this was 2008; she had just run for president and was now slated to become the secretary of state. I had attended a fundraiser a few years earlier for Hillary in a neighbor's living room and was able to hear her speak passionately about families, health care, and her commitment to be a voice for those who do not have a voice in our society, people like Bobby. I doubted she got involved in such small matters concerning one person in Syracuse, but what did I know? None of my plans had amounted to anything as of yet.

"We can try," Bobby said, his brown eyes full of hope.

He had done everything I had asked of him, so I wrote the letter to Hillary.

July 7, 2008

Senator Hillary Rodham Clinton
780 Third Ave.
Suite 2601
New York, NY 10017

Dear Senator Clinton:

I am writing this letter on behalf of my brother, Robert Bargabos. My brother suffers from multiple disabilities. He has a low IQ (72), learning disabilities, fetal alcohol syndrome, and narcolepsy. Because of his intellectual disability, I try to take care of his business affairs— doctor's appointments, legal matters, financial matters, etc. I am writing this with his knowledge and permission. Please accept this letter on his behalf.

I am asking for your help with the Social Security Administration. Robert applied for Social Security disability and was denied benefits on March 3, 2008. What frustrates me the most is that it is quite obvious in the denial letter that they missed the primary disability and cite misinformation and incorrect conclusions for denying Robert disability benefits. Our only recourse is to request a hearing with the SSA. We have retained an attorney and filed a request for a hearing on April 8, 2008. I have spoken with the Office of Disability Adjudication and Review, and they have confirmed that they received our hearing request and that the wait time is 18–24 months. This seems extremely unfair and unreasonable, especially since their determination was based on incorrect conclusions.

Robert wants to work and be independent and productive in our society, but because of his narcolepsy, FAS, and the resulting limitations and learning disabilities, he is unable to support himself. He needs help. His need for services and support has been recognized and documented by other experts/agencies—VESID, BOCES, The Arc evaluation, and his doctors. I would like a hearing as soon as possible based on financial hardship and the fact that the initial review and decision was clearly erroneous. The decision cites an "emotional problem," "alcoholism," and a "sleeping problem." The team that reviewed the case completely missed that he is not the alcoholic, but rather a victim of fetal alcohol syndrome, and they describe narcolepsy as a "sleeping problem." These assumptions and conclusions are outrageous, and performance at this level is unacceptable by a government agency.

I appreciate you doing anything you can to help with this matter. Please contact me with any questions.

Thank you.
Kelly Bargabos

I faxed the letter to Hillary's office; regular mail would be too slow. Two days later, we received a letter back from her office assuring us that she had contacted the appropriate officials. Bobby was hopeful; I hoped Bobby was right.

July 9, 2008, two days after we sent the letter to Hillary asking for her help, the phone beside my bed rang, knocking me out of my dream. My heart thumped in my ears, my hands shook in a panic, like they do when your phone rings in the middle of the night. My still-sleeping mind and eyes tried to figure out the number on the caller ID. It was one I'd never seen before.

"Hello?"

"Kell?" The voice was familiar.

"My house burned," Bobby said.

NIGHTMARE

Bobby

I pulled my head up off the desk and struggled to open my heavy eyes. A distant, muffled alarm woke me up. It wasn't the song I was listening to. No, the music had stopped. It wasn't coming from outside. The sound was relentless. The air was thick. I smelled a woodstove burning. I couldn't breathe. Something was wrong. I took my headphones off and got up from the desk. I heard snapping and crackling. What was that noise? I walked out of my bedroom, turned right toward the kitchen. The wall behind my stove was engulfed in flames. I couldn't remember if I'd left the stove on. I thought dinner was in the microwave.

Four hours before, I'd come home from work and visited with my neighbors for a while in the warm July air before asking my one neighbor, Matt, to take me to the grocery store. When we got home, Matt went upstairs; I went to my place, right below him. While I waited for dinner, I went in my room, turned on my headphones and the television. I didn't mean to fall asleep. I never did. It'd been almost a year since I was diagnosed with narcolepsy. It had started about six years before that, when I was twenty-six or twen-

ty-seven. I was working at the casino then as a beverage porter, making sure the server area was stocked with drinks. One night, my legs gave out and the tray of drinks I was carrying smashed to the ground. It scared me. After that, people started telling me it seemed like I slurred my words and my eyes were half closed most of the time. My mom thought I was stoned or drunk. I couldn't help it. And I couldn't explain it. I didn't know why it was happening. Not long after that, I was at my mom's for a family dinner. I was laughing at a joke, and then I fell against the dryer. Then, at dad's birthday party, when the whole family was playing kickball, I fell when it was my turn to run. Seemed to happen when I got excited or nervous, and sometimes for no reason at all. Just kept happening more and more. I went to a sleep lab at nine o'clock for the test. I was nervous about staying there all night. When they called my name, two guys came to get me. Walking down the hallway, my legs gave out and I fell on top of them. The nurses panicked and called for help. Kelly told them about the cataplexy. At least the doctor finally saw that I had narcolepsy. I thought maybe I'd get some help after that.

Hot yellow-and-orange flames blistered the kitchen walls, threatening me, it seemed like. Smoke filled my mouth and burned my eyes. My legs couldn't move as fast as my pounding heart or my panicked mind told me to. Move! I lumbered to the door and fumbled with the security bar propped beneath the doorknob. It took me some time, too much time, to get the security bar out and open the door. I thought about Matt. I should have tried to get him out, should have run up the stairs instead of down, should have tried helping him. I was mad at myself for not using my training to put the fire out. I'd been a member of the Hinsdale Fire Department. I never fought any fires, they wouldn't let me. I remembered some of the training though. I'd *ridden along on calls. But I ran down the stairs, out the front door, and into the parking lot instead. That still haunts me.*

I stood outside with my neighbors and watched my home go up in flames. I had a hard time understanding what was happening. I borrowed a cell phone to call my parents and my sisters. "My house burned," I said. Somebody gave me a pair of sandals to put on my bare feet. My parents and sisters came right away and stood with me. We watched the firemen toss my furniture out the picture window of my apartment. Everything I owned, everything I loved was in there— the Syracuse Crunch jerseys Kevin gave me, my television, my CDs, my Matchbox car collection, my Hess Truck collection. Everything that made me happy, the things I'd worked hard for, the treasures that gave me comfort when I was alone at night—destroyed. I choked down a sob that tried to escape. My legs gave out and I fell.

Someone said, "It's a miracle his daughter wasn't there."

"Good thing he had that smoke alarm."

"I heard he had headphones on. It's a miracle he heard the alarm."

"Thank God the firemen got Matt out."

"Did you see him trapped up against the window? I hope he's okay."

"Bobby's lucky to be alive."

I didn't say anything. It wasn't the first time narcolepsy had tried to kill me.

The year before, I'd worked the second shift at the hotel, cleaning rooms and doing other maintenance jobs. It was after eleven when I made the short drive home. My eyes closed, and it wasn't long before I drifted off the road and into the center ditch between the two sides of the highway. I drove full-speed into a street sign. It pierced my windshield on the driver's side, where my head would have been if I'd been awake. It shot straight through the car and out the rear window.

The fact that I would never drive again bothers me the most. I have to depend on family and friends for rides to the grocery store. I had cataplexy on my bike and fell into the ditch and hit my head. I had to start taking the bus to work, and I hated it. The young kids laughed at me when I nodded off in my seat, spilling my coffee, and dropping my papers. When the driver woke me up at the end of the line and kicked me off the bus, I had to find my way home. It had been so hard for me to get my license in the first place. I didn't get it until I was back from Binghamton and in my twenties. It took two tries to pass the written test, and when I passed the driving test, I finally felt like everybody else. Now that was gone.

An EMT from the ambulance checked on me. The Red Cross gave me a voucher for one hundred dollars. My sisters and mother came back a week later, after the fire department declared it was safe. They stepped around the holes in the floor and the soot-covered remnants of my world. They gagged on the smell of waterlogged, rotting garbage. They knew they could never get the stench or the black soot off my things. They rescued two picture albums, my metal box of important papers, and my Matchbox cars.

Four years later, when the landlord sued me for damages, I was questioned under oath and still couldn't remember what happened the night of the fire. They said I told the building super at the time that I'd left a pan of fish frying on the stove. The jury convicted me of unattended cooking and told me I had to pay half a million dollars to the insurance company, even though they knew I had nothing. I'd carry this debt for the rest of my life. The only debt I had. I knew I could never pay it off. But that doesn't bother me as much as being blamed. That, too, still haunts my days.

In my new apartment Kelly installed fire extinguisher cans above my stove. She bought me a microwave that can bake and broil and asked me to cook everything in there, even though she knew I wouldn't. I wasn't allowed to fry fish anymore.

Narcolepsy doesn't leave me alone. It hovers over me, like a thief waiting to steal any chance of the normal life I dreamt of. I can't fight it; I tried. It's stronger than me. Made me sleep when I was cooking, eating, talking, working, riding in a car, on a bike, or on a bus. Made people think I was stoned or drunk when I wasn't. Made me fall over when I was in a chair, in bed, standing still, left me broken and bruised with rug burns on my face, purple gouges in my side, and black eyes. Made me see things that weren't there, taunting and teasing me, making me think I was crazy.

Narcolepsy keeps me in this nightmare where I'm never fully awake and where peaceful sleep does not exist. My dream of having my own corner of the world—my grass to mow, my flowers to plant, my driveway to shovel, my home—died a little more each day.

PART THREE

FOUND

THANK YOU, HILLARY

BOBBY IS A SURVIVOR. IF I'D LEARNED NOTHING else over the last thirty-some-odd years, it is that. He survived his mother's womb, the beatings and scalding baths, her cigarette burns—getting out of her home just in time. He's survived his own mistakes and bad decisions, the streets, and now this fire—getting out of his home just in time. After the rescue trucks left and the neighbors shuffled back to their apartments, Bobby went home with a friend to sleep on his couch. I went home and tried to sleep, but when I closed my eyes I saw Bobby asleep at his desk, flames raging in the kitchen. What if the smoke alarms hadn't woken him up? How terrified he must have been to experience the panic of death, if even for a moment. What if he hadn't been able to get his door open? I yanked my mind away from these images by thanking God for saving Bobby again, focusing on the miracle instead of what could have been.

Most days, it seemed like there was a force outside of Bobby trying to take him out of this life. Yet despite my worry for him and about him, he had a way of making it—of being okay. An equal and opposite force for good in Bobby's life had kept him alive all these years. For every person who pretended to be a friend while they conned him out of the money in his pocket, or conned him into stealing or driving the getaway car, for every predator, there was a friend with a couch that he could sleep on when he had nowhere else to go, a friend with a hot meal or a ride to the store. These people had been answers to my daily prayers.

When I had opportunities to help people, I returned the favor. One night, Kevin and I saw a teenage girl crying on the side of the road, her car in the ditch. We gave her a ride to her parents' house, thirty miles out of our way; I imagined we were their answered prayer. I gave twenty dollars to the guy in the convenience store parking lot who convinced me that his car was on the side of the road and he needed this money to get home. Another time, after filling my own car at the pump, I filled up a portable gas can for the man who looked like his car was his home. I wondered if he had a sister worrying about him.

The fire became a new marker in Bobby's life. When did you start your job at Express Mart? "After the fire." What year did you move to Hudson Street? "After the fire." Did you work at the bakery before or after? "Before." It also became a symbol for lost things. What happened to your NASCAR jacket, your dress shoes, the sweatshirt you bought your daughter on vacation last year in the Outer Banks? "Lost in the fire."

More desperate than ever to get Bobby the help he needed, I sent another letter to the SSA office explaining that his home had been destroyed. I faxed them a copy of the newspaper article and detailed his situation. He'd lost all of his personal belongings, as well as a place to live. Due to his lack of resources he would be unable to recoup any of it or secure a new apartment. I begged the woman on the phone to classify him as a critical case and move up the hearing. She promised to try.

I still needed supporting documentation from his neurologist for the disability hearing. I took Bobby to his appointment with Dr. Tran at the neurology clinic at Upstate University Hospital. The waiting room was a big open space with chairs lining the walls and a row of chairs back-to-back down the middle. Almost every seat was filled with old people, parents holding crying babies, men and women my age, teenagers. Their chatter bounced off the walls and added to our anxiety. Bobby and I found two chairs across from each other and waited, nervously. We both knew how important it was to get the doctor's support.

Not long after our scheduled appointment time of 3:30, we were called into the examining room. I skimmed neurology literature and read the pamphlet about traumatic brain injury at least three times while Bobby slept in his chair. An hour passed before the doctor walked in. He was young with dark hair and glasses. I began reading him my notepad list of cataplexy attacks, describing how Bobby couldn't move or speak, and that they're happening more and more. The doctor took notes while I told him about the fire and about the time Bobby was riding his bike down South Bay Road when he started to tremble. He had felt it coming on and was able to aim his bike into the ditch before he fell over; he knew enough to get himself out of traffic. I also told him I thought Bobby was starting to hallucinate. After fifteen minutes, the doctor cut me off. "I have to see another patient. I'll be right back." He walked out of the room. Bobby and I looked at each other and shrugged. It wasn't long before his head bowed, fast asleep again in the chair. I stared at the clock and bounced my legs, tapped my fingers, sighed loudly, and every time the clock ticked, another minute passed and my blood pressure pounded upward.

After another hour, the young doctor and his supervisor swung open the door and whirled into the room engrossed in a conversation with each other. I kicked at Bobby's feet to wake him up. Before the supervisor introduced herself or greeted Bobby, she turned to me. "The only thing we can do is have your brother admitted to the hospital so we can observe these seizures."

"I'm not sure that will work," I said. "How will he…"

"I have been trained by the Mayo Clinic; I'm an expert. I know what I'm doing." It was obvious she wasn't looking for my input. I was trying to tell her I didn't think Bobby would have cataplexy attacks lying in a hospital bed. How could his legs give out if he was lying down?

"He just had an EEG done at Crouse Hospital. University was too busy to do it, so they sent us there. I asked them to send you the report."

"This report is meaningless to me. I am too busy to read reports from other hospitals."

"Are you kidding me? Guess what? I'm busy too, so is Bobby, and our time is valuable. We've been in this examining room for over two hours!"

"I'm sorry about that," the supervisor said as she and the other doctor opened the door and started to walk out.

"Wait." I stood up. They stopped mid-doorway and turned to look at me. "I need a form filled out for Bobby's disability hearing. He's been denied and we're appealing…"

"It's my personal policy not to fill out forms." She proceeded to tell me that she didn't know Bobby well enough and we should take him to somebody else.

"Somebody else? You're his doctor." She looked at me. "He needs this in order to get his disability approved," I explained. "They don't take testimony from family members. We don't have time to start over with another doctor."

"I will dictate strongly in the notes that we support his disability. The notes are Robert's property. He can get them anytime." She turned and left the examining room with Dr. Tran right behind her. Nothing was said about Bobby's medical condition, any follow up, or what the next steps were. They hadn't examined Bobby; they didn't even speak to him.

I looked at the clock. It was after 6:00 p.m. The waiting room was empty. The office staff had gone home. There was no one I could ask for copies of his file or notes from the doctor. I dropped Bobby off at my parents' house, reassuring him that we'd figure something out. That night, before I changed into my pajamas or had dinner, I sat at my computer and typed a two-page letter to the patient relations department at Upstate University Hospital. My fingers flew across the keys, my fury expelled onto the page with every stroke. I described the doctor's appointment, how they were argumentative and resistant to questions, that neither one of them physically examined Bobby. I said that it was completely unacceptable and unfair to refuse to fill out disability forms that are required by the government, especially when she was an expert in neurological disorders. I told them I felt the treatment my brother experienced was substandard and unprofessional and that I couldn't help but wonder if it was because Bobby is a Medicaid patient. Whatever the reason, it was intolerable and disappointing.

I faxed the letter the next day. Two hours later the supervising doctor called. She said she was shocked and humiliated by my letter. She was "way too hurt" to be effective attending to Bobby in the future, so she was handing him off to one of her colleagues. I explained to her that it was not my intent to be personally hurtful but that we have been frustrated for years and struggling to get people to pay attention. "You have our attention now," she said.

"Will you fill out the disability form?"

"The risk management department has issued a policy that prevents me from filling out forms like these, but I will write a letter strongly supporting your brother's need for disability." I thanked her and hung up, satisfied but still disturbed by the flagrant discrimination that must occur every day for hundreds, maybe thousands of people. I couldn't understand how people like my brother were able to overcome this or how they could possibly wade through all of the required paperwork and procedures without an advocate, somebody that could fight for them and demand they be seen and heard. I could not let it happen without telling somebody that it was wrong; it shouldn't be this way.

Within a matter of days, I received the letter she promised me supporting Bobby's appeal for disability benefits. I faxed it immediately to the lawyer. I had been emailing the lawyer's office on a weekly basis to get status updates on Bobby's hearing. This really pissed off my sister.

"You're embarrassing me," she told me.

"Why? I ask for status updates from the people who work for me all the time."

"You're pushy and demanding. You're a lawyer's worst nightmare."

"I don't care. I'm their customer, or actually Bobby is. They're getting paid." I didn't care who got mad at me. Bobby's life was at stake. All the rest was insignificant.

I had come to believe that there are things in this lifetime which have eternal significance, and there are things that do not. How we interact with the people we know and the new ones we meet, how we care for those who need help has an everlasting impact. If the basic needs of a person's spirit, soul, and body are met, it allows them the ability to keep their own corner of the world—their home—safe and prosperous for themselves and their family. This is all there is.

Six weeks after the fire, at the end of August, we received a new decision on Bobby's disability claim. The SSA office contacted me directly, and the lawyer's office emailed me the good news. But it wasn't until I actually held the report in my hand, and saw the words "fully favorable" decision, that the lead weight attached to my body and mind was cut loose. The burden of this fight disappeared into the distance, and the space previously occupied by this heavy load filled instantly with fresh air. There would still be a lifetime of things to do for Bobby—we had to find him a new home and furnishings, a new job, doctors who might actually treat his narcolepsy—but *this* battle had been won. It was worth every minute, every hour, every phone call, every letter, every argument with the doctors, my sister, the lawyer, the SSA—all worth it.

Bobby was convinced he owed it all to Hillary. Her office had sent us a follow-up letter, including copies of the correspondence between her office and the SSA, proving that she did contact them on Bobby's behalf. His disability claim was approved thirty days after her letter. I don't know if Hillary personally saw any of this; I assume one of her staff members did the work. I didn't tell Bobby that at the time and never will. I don't know if it was her letter, or the fire, or the letter we fought to get from the neurologist that spurred the approval of his claim. It doesn't matter. Bobby believes it was Hillary, and that is good enough for me.

A few months later Bobby wrote her a thank you note. This time I sent the letter to Washington, DC, as she was now secretary of state. A letter came back from her office with an eight-by-ten framed and autographed portrait. It has been hanging on his wall ever since.

2/9/09

Dear Secretary of State Hillary Clinton. First of all I would like to Congratulations on your New Job. I am wright you this letter. Becuse I want to thank you For the quick response to the letter that my sister wrote to you when you were Senator.

My Name is Robert Bargabos and my sister name is Kelly Bargabos. Kelly had wrote to you about my SSD.

I was Diagnosis with a Learing Disability, Narcolepsy and Sleep Apnea it was verer Helpfull to me I now get my SSD. all thank's to you and my Sister. it has Been hard for me But my siter helpa me out a lot armd my mom and dad do too.

Befor I got your 2nd letter. Back in July I Just head a Apt. Fire and lost every thing But I got out and Now I am getting Back on my feet. I hope you Like your New Job and I think you will Be good at it. I do have one more thing to ask you I alway's wanted to meet the President of the united states and also I want to meet you and Bill and shake your hand. Could you see what you can do for me well I Know you Have thing to do so thank you for your Help

Robert
Bargabos

TREASURE

I'M IN!" I YELLED.

I was standing in my hallway, in front of the new picture that hung on the wall. It was a psychedelic, random pattern of different shapes and shades of brown and orange. The trick was to stand in the right spot, not too far or too near. You had to be just the right distance from it, and then fix your eyes at the center of the pattern and wait. We'd yell, "I'm in!" when our eyes adjusted and we were able to see the image hidden within the pattern. A shipwreck lay cockeyed at the bottom of the ocean in the midst of a coral reef. Plant life had taken over what remained of the ship, the boards worn and faded by the briny water. A treasure chest had burst open when it slammed into the sandy floor and gold coins and pearl necklaces were spilling over the top and down the side. A peaceful looking shark swam in and out of the ship's windows. Kevin could always "get in" faster than me; I had a hard time. We paraded everyone that visited our home in front of the picture to see if they could "get in." The trick was being still long enough to let your eyes see what was there.

Bobby settled into a one-bedroom apartment above a garage with an old bed from my parents; a kitchen table with four chairs donated by my sister; and dishes, pots, and pans left by the previous tenant. With his disability compensation he was able to buy a new couch. He took care of the place like it was his own—swept the driveway, mowed the lawn, made sure the garbage cans were out on Tuesday night and back in the garage Wednesday morning. He asked me to be his representative payee once he began receiving disability. His monthly check would be deposited into my account, and I would pay his rent, cable bill, and phone bill. He kept any money he made shoveling snow, mowing lawns, or from the new job VESID had helped him find. He worked ten hours a week at a convenience store sweeping the parking lot and cleaning gas pumps and the bays of the car wash. The store manager was good to Bobby. She was patient with his drowsiness and saw his work ethic and honest character as an asset. Bobby's favorite part of the job was cleaning out the vacuum cleaner outside the car wash bay. He's found winning scratch off lottery tickets, gift cards with small balances left on them, an iPod Nano, a gold ring, pennies, nickels, dimes, and quarters—treasures.

Bobby has a knack for finding treasure in what other people consider garbage or junk. He's found these treasures in pawnshops and by the side of the road. He loves to go "curbing," searching through the random things that people leave in front of their house with a "free" sign. Over time, he put shelves up on his new walls and filled them with collectible glasses—Ronald McDonald, Grimace, Fred Flintstone, Shrek; ceramic bears and dogs; pictures of his daughter and his brother and sisters and their families; Hess Trucks and Matchbox cars. He found a shelf with a clock in the middle that didn't work and positioned the hands at two o'clock to "make it look like it worked" and hung it up on his wall. He found end tables and other furniture that he stripped, sanded, and stained. His favorite finds were electronics—CD players, televisions, vacuum cleaners—which he could usually get working, and then he'd sell them. He used the workbench in the garage to tinker with the things he found. His "curbing" used to embarrass me, and his spending money on junk frustrated me. A few years before, I was on the couch watching television, half-listening to Bobby on the phone, when he started to tell me about the great deal he got on a used stereo and speakers for twenty-five dollars at the thrift store.

"Bob! Why? Why would you spend your money on a stereo? You already have two." I rolled my eyes and threw my head back in frustration.

"Yeah, but this one was nicer. Once I get it working, I'll sell the other two."

"Don't you think you should save your money for groceries or rent?"

"You know, with the small life I have, things like this make me happy."

Moments like those began to stop me in my tracks. I called them "Playground Moments." Moments when I realized, usually after I'd messed up, that I was behaving like those kids on the merry-go-round, trying to get someone, usually Bobby, to behave like me. To run like me, spend like me, live like me, to live a "normal" life, to do what's expected. I began to catch myself in the middle of those moments, like when I skidded into the express lane at the grocery store, frustrated to find someone ahead of me who I could see would slow me down. Someone older, someone who had to set a cane down to count his money, or just some lonely person whose only conversation that day would be with the cashier and so they took their time. Bobby taught me that I shouldn't judge different-sized lives than mine.

⁓

If my brother was slow before, narcolepsy would make sure he'd never get on the merry-go-round, crippling his body and mind in a way he and I didn't imagine possible. We found a new neurologist and changed his general practitioner two or three times until we found one that took Medicaid *and* seemed to care about Bobby's health, which was no small task. He began taking more than just Provigil to manage his symptoms; he took Vivactil for the cataplexy and Seroquel and clonazepam to help him sleep. Doctors continued trying to find just the right mix of drugs, which is all they seem to know to do with narcolepsy. I looked for a support group in our area but none existed. I promised Bobby we'd start our own someday. There had to be others like him suffering with this nightmare.

He had started to get better at sensing when a cataplexy attack was coming and tried to avoid falling. One night he called me about nine o'clock.

"Where have you been? I called you a couple of times," I said. I had called him a few times throughout the day, and he didn't answer. I always worried when I couldn't reach him.

"I couldn't get up," he told me.

"Why not?"

"Afraid I would fall."

"Where?"

"I was sitting at my computer desk and felt like I was going to have one of my attacks."

"What did you do?"

"I stayed in my chair. I waited for it to go away, but I got really tired after a while so I crawled to my bed."

As much as he tried to outsmart cataplexy, it still caught him off guard. One time Kevin took Bobby shopping in Walmart. They stood in the electronics department looking at cameras in the display case. "What do think about these?" Kevin said. "Do you like the blue or green one? I like the blue but the green one is ten dollars cheaper." Kevin looked to his left where Bobby had been standing. "Bob?" He looked behind him. "Bob?" Kevin looked down. Bobby was lying on his side, almost in a fetal position, his body jerking as though being electrocuted, his eyes back in his head.

"Code Red. Code Red," the cashier called on his radio. Within minutes they were swarmed by blue-vested workers.

"Call 911," someone yelled.

"No, no, he's okay. He'll be okay." Kevin convinced them to cancel the code red. "He's not having a heart attack," he told them. Somebody got a chair. Kevin and a blue vest helped Bobby up off the floor. They gave him a bottle of water and a wet washcloth. Bobby, drained and silent, sat in the chair, waiting for the strength to stand up.

I ordered him a medical ID necklace with a tag that read NARCOLEPSY PATIENT. In case of emergency, I listed my cell phone and Kevin's cell phone. One evening, he walked to the store to buy milk with the neighbor's thirteen-year-old daughter. The girl, her father, and brother were close friends of his and spent a lot of time with him. Bobby was at the counter paying for his milk when his legs gave out and he fell over. The cashier and another customer rushed to his side, wanting to call an ambulance. The girl reassured them without flinching, "He's fine. He does this all the time."

Not long after he moved into his new apartment, Bobby started wrestling with unidentified creatures. Some kind of furry rodent, a rat or raccoon perhaps, taunted and teased him while he slept, biting his toes and pulling at his blanket.

Hallucinations are a somewhat less common symptom of narcolepsy, and they can happen when falling asleep or waking up—hypnagogic hallucinations when going to bed and hypnopompic hallucinations upon awakening. Whatever the technical term, they were vivid and frightening.

"There's something in my apartment," Bobby told me.

"What do you mean there's something in your apartment?"

"There's an animal or something under my bed."

"What's it look like?"

"I dunno. I haven't seen it."

"Well, if you haven't seen it, how do you know something is there?"

"Because. It bites my toes."

"Do you see it when it bites your toes?"

"No. But it has a big tail."

This conversation went on for months. Bobby described how he could feel something living in his mattress. When he was in bed, he felt something scurry around underneath him. Sometimes the critter would nibble on his toes when he was sleeping or try to pull his blanket off him. He felt something living in his couch too. He told my mother and Kevin the same stories. I explained to them that hallucinations are part of narcolepsy. I found other people with similar stories on the Internet, but Bobby was convinced his were real. We were doubtful but at the same time thought it could have been possible. He lived in an old house, and he wasn't always the best housekeeper so mice were a possibility. He had a yard with squirrels and other wildlife that could have made their way into his bedroom.

One Saturday, Kevin and I went to his apartment to check it out for ourselves. We stripped the sheets and blankets off his mattress, flipped it over, end to end, looking for holes of entry and exit. We picked up the box spring. There were no signs of an animal, but Bobby was still convinced it was inside. Kevin ripped the thin, white felt covering off the bottom to prove it was empty. When we looked under his couch and refrigerator, we found pieces of candy and chocolate and looked at Bobby. "I left those out to see if he would eat 'em." There were no telltale signs of mouse droppings or any other kind of feces. There were no nests. We bought six boxes of d-Con and placed them in corners. They were never touched.

This creature continued to haunt him. I hired a professional exterminator, hoping he could get the rodent out of Bobby's mind. Kevin met him early one morning. He walked around the small apartment first. Then, on his hands and knees, he scanned the floorboards around the living room, bedroom, dining room, and kitchen. He lay on his belly and looked under the couch, the bed, behind the refrigerator. He shone his flashlight in closets and the attic. He came to the same conclusion we did. There was nothing there.

I should have been relieved, but I wasn't. I would rather he had found some furry creature with giant teeth living in Bobby's mattress than have to explain to him that none of it was true, that he was just being tortured by his imagination. Every once in a while after that day, Bobby would mention his creature to me in a conversation and we'd joke about it. I knew he still saw it.

Bobby lives alone and battles his illness by himself most of the time. He is almost always alone when he falls or when he sees things that aren't there. We talked about getting him guardrails for his bed, but instead he took his mattress off the frame so that it's closer to the floor if he falls. We tried to move his furniture so there's less for him to bang into. One time he fell asleep drying himself off after a shower, falling face first into the sink. We've talked about getting him a chair or bench for the shower, but I'm afraid then he'll certainly fall asleep in there. We settled on a grab bar for the tub. His injuries so far include gashes in his side, deep purple bruises, black eyes, bruised ribs, and fractured bones around his right eye. He hits his head often, and we never really know the kind of impact that could have. We mentioned this to his visiting nurse, and she told us that a lot of her patients with narcolepsy and cataplexy wear a helmet to protect themselves.

Narcolepsy is a bastard. I hate it. I hate that with all Bobby has survived, narcolepsy will continue to try to take his life. I hate that I haven't found a way to beat it yet. Still, Bobby isn't bitter. He keeps moving. He continues to work, makes friends with his neighbors, shovels snow, and cares for his landlord. He doesn't give up on his dreams of going to Nashville and the Grand Ole Opry or of owning his own home.

I asked Bobby to help me write this story. His price: dinner. I asked him questions and read him pages, and he answered between bites, helping me with the details. One night, between swigs of my chocolate milkshake and bites of french fries, I asked my brother, "Bob, what do you want people to know about you? What do *you* want people to know?" I waited for him to answer while he finished chewing his barbecue chicken sandwich. He was a notoriously slow eater. He savored every single bite. I was done at least fifteen minutes before him; that's how it always was with him. He was the last one eating, the last one to put his fork down, the last one at the table, at every single meal. He took his time when it came to food.

I waited as he took a sip of his orange Creamsicle shake. When he was done, he looked up at me and told me as sure as anything, "That I'm not a disease."

I'm in.

...the mirror

IT'S BEEN ALMOST TWO YEARS." I LOOKED OVER AT DR. Marsha sitting in her armchair. No reaction. This woman could be a poker champion. I needed some sort of validation from her. Kevin and I had been laboring through two years of therapy, together and in solo sessions like today, to try and heal our marriage and each other. Kevin had worked on his issues. He worked hard. I knew it was difficult for him to dredge up old hurts—to scratch open scars that had been sealed a long time ago. It was hard for him to come to terms with his childhood and all that had happened to him to make him the person he was now. I witnessed his pain. It was real. It was important. Unexpectedly though, I had discovered many things about myself, my motivations, the reasons why I was the way I was. I wished I had learned these things twenty years earlier. I was sure I would have made different choices if I had understood the reasons why.

I needed to know from Dr. Marsha if we were on track, if I was making progress, and if all the tears and pain and self-scrutiny had been worth it. *Would it make a difference?*

"Two years. How does that make you feel?" she finally asked.

"I don't know. I still have resentment, sadness, anger."

"That is not unusual."

"It just feels like I should be over it by now," I said, "and moving on. Kevin is making progress and trying to move on. I feel bad that I haven't yet. Like I'm holding him back. I feel bad that I don't love him as much as I used to."

"Those are huge red flags, Kelly. You can't decide those things for Kevin, only he can. And you are the only one who can decide it for you. Is his love enough for you to move forward? And is your love enough for him?" she asked.

I shifted uncomfortably on the sofa and picked up the pillow from the end of the couch, not returning her gaze or answering her questions. At this point, Kevin and I were still together, trying to let this process of therapy and time heal our wounds.

"It seems to me that you're falling into your habit of thinking of others first, worrying about Kevin's feelings instead of your own. I'd rather leave those conversations for our joint sessions and just talk about you, Kelly."

"I have consciously been trying to be more selfish," I said, sounding a little more defensive than I had intended.

"I prefer the term self-focused," she said. "Selfish has negative connotations. It is not negative to put yourself first."

That was news to me.

"And it's not just with Kevin. You do it at work. You do it with your family, with everything." She continued, "Let me give you an example. I see you as someone who chose not to have children yet doesn't allow herself to experience any of the benefits of that."

"What do you mean?" I asked. I was intrigued to see where she was going with this.

"You're suffering the pain and emptiness of not having children but none of the real freedom and benefits," she said.

She was right. When people found out I didn't have children, they often said to me, "Must be nice to have all that free time." I never told them about the meals I served at the soup kitchen, or the children I taught at my church for seventeen years, or that I took my niece school shopping every fall and went to her teacher conferences because her parents can't or won't, or how I took my brother to his doctor's appointments and paid his bills. I never told them that I have less free time than most people I know.

"You know what I think?" Dr. Marsha asked.

"What's that?"

"I think you're a people-pleaser."

We talked about her theory for the rest of that session. She believed that I based my emotions and actions upon what other people wanted of me. She said it was like I saw myself through a distorted lens, like a funhouse mirror. I thought I was looking at myself, but I really wasn't. I was looking at what other people needed of me, what other people wanted me to do, to be, and I obliged. I would become whatever they needed me to be.

"Kelly, what do you get out of all this?" her eyes pointing at me as if they already knew the answer.

"What do you mean?" I asked, confused, still reeling from everything she had just said.

"People-pleasing. You must get something out of it," Dr. Marsha said.

"I guess it makes me happy." I looked at the clock on the table, hoping this session was almost over.

People liked me. They accepted me in this role. I must have needed that love and acceptance and thought I could only get it if I played along. Would anybody need me or want me if I wasn't so agreeable?

The problem with this behavior is that even when I got this love and acceptance, it didn't satisfy me because I was angry that I had to betray myself to get it. I wasn't living true to my authentic self, and that made me angry.

People-pleasing is a vain pursuit, an empty quest. It's like looking for happiness in drugs or alcohol. The happiness is temporary, not lasting, and only as good as the next crisis in somebody else's life. I always thought I just had an altruistic nature to save the world and those around me. It turns out that I needed to save the world in order for me to be happy when I came home at night, when I went to bed, or sat on my couch. I couldn't relax until everyone was where they were supposed to be, doing what they were supposed to do.

My image of myself was so warped by the needs, feelings, and problems of other people that I didn't know what *I* really looked like anymore. I had spent so much of my life worrying about everyone else—being in tune with what others were feeling, and doing everything I could to make everyone happy—I had lost myself in the process. What did I really want? What made me happy? What did I want out of this marriage? This life? *Could I remove the distorted lenses through which I saw myself?*

Dr. Marsha helped me see clearly that at the end of my life, I would either have integrity or despair. Integrity that I had been authentic to my true self or despair that my life was over and I never found me!

Maybe this is why I had always felt panicked about not finding the life I should be living—it's not my life I was looking for, it was me!

FAR FROM HOME

I'M LOST," BOBBY SAID.

"What do you mean, you're lost?"

"I'm lost." His voice had an edge to it. This wasn't going to be our usual checking-in-at-the-end-of-the-day phone call.

"Start at the beginning, Bob."

"I fell asleep on the bus." This wasn't the first time; it happened all the time. Sometimes he fell out of his seat, jarred awake by landing in the aisle, and sometimes he slept right through his stop. But it was usually after the downtown transfer, and he'd be on his regular route at least. When he sleeps through his regular stop, the driver will kick him off at the end of the line, and he walks the mile or so home.

"Where are you now?"

"I don't know. Grand Avenue, I think. I'm at a store, Geddes Express."

I had heard of that store in the news, usually associated with a drive-by shooting. I think someone was killed in the parking lot a few years before. I knew of Grand Avenue, but it ran through the entire west side of the city. "Where are you on Grand Avenue?"

"I don't know."

"Are you near a corner? Look for another street sign." His breath was fast and heavy as he looked around for a cross street.

"Oh, here's one. S-h-o-n-n-a-r..."

"Shonnard Street? You're on Shonnard Street?"

"I guess. How far am I from home?"

"Stay where you are. I'll come get you."

I wasn't exactly sure where the two streets intersected, so I got on Shonnard at the beginning and drove west, searching the darkness for this corner store. It seemed like all the street lights were out; the streets were empty or at least appeared to be. The homes that lined both sides of Shonnard, once grand with majestic front porches, neat lawns, and stately doors and windows were now abandoned, left for dead, boarded-up homes, rumored to be used by drug dealers as crack houses.

I pulled up to a stoplight, and on my right was the store I was looking for. I spotted Bobby standing on the sidewalk in front, wearing his green safety vest he bought recently. I always told him, "You shouldn't walk after dark in dark clothes, drivers can't see you. It's dangerous. Please be careful walking home." So he bought the vest.

I tapped my horn and Bobby looked up. His eyes were wide, and he walked to my car like his life depended on it. I saw relief on his face as he jumped in and explained what had happened, sweat running off him even though it was a cold November night. He told me how he had fallen asleep on the bus ride home from work and slept through his downtown transfer, ending up on the wrong route. He woke up in a neighborhood he didn't recognize, panicked, and got off at the next stop, realizing then he had no idea how to get home.

Bobby's quiet neighborhood was filled with small two- and three-bedroom ranch or split-level homes that were brand new fifty or so years ago, with wood siding in shades of brown and blue, most needing a fresh coat of paint. They sat hopeful that one day they would house young families again, just starting out, with children to run and play in their small yards. Bobby liked his neighborhood. The retired woman on the corner gave him rides to the store and let him bum cigarettes. He noticed For Sale signs on front yards and told me about the house and what he'd heard about it from the neighbors. He still wanted his own home.

I saw an ad for a non-profit group, Home HeadQuarters, which helps people buy their first home. Bobby and I attended a forty-five-minute orientation to see if it would be a solution for him. I realized after the first few minutes that it wasn't. The $215 fee for the first-time homebuyer course was feasible, but the ten-hour written course was not. After the seminar, I had a private conversation with the woman in charge. I asked if I could take the course for him. Could I apply on his behalf with him living in the house? Unfortunately, the answer was no. The home had to be owner occupied. That was when I knew he would never own his own home. But I never told him that.

I pulled into his driveway. He got out of the car, walked around to my side, and rested his arm on my door, leaning in my window.

"Someone was in my garage again last night."

He had told me about the guy that's been hanging out in his garage in the middle of the night. He had mentioned it to me on the phone two days ago. Bobby had woken up at 4:00 a.m. and heard someone outside his door. He yelled to scare off the invader and was convinced he heard a coat rustling. "Do you think it's hallucinations, Bob? You know they're part of narcolepsy."

"No, I'm telling you, somebody was out there."

"Okay, well, keep your door locked. I'm sure whoever it was won't be back. Have a good night." I knew he had started sleeping with a baseball bat in the middle of his bed. When would his hallucinations make him lose his mind?

"Okay. Thanks for the ride."

I waited in my car while he fumbled with his keys and unlocked his door. When would the day come when he'd wake up in some unknown neighborhood and not be able to reach me to come pick him up? Would someone beat him and steal his phone or his cash? I waited until he walked up the stairs and unlocked his apartment door. When would he fall and hit is head so hard it would knock him out, or worse? Once I saw his living room light turn on, I knew he was safe for now and I left.

GROUP HOME

I PULLED INTO BOBBY'S DRIVEWAY, STOPPING JUST A few feet from his overhead garage door. I was there to take him to a doctor's appointment. I could see him, his big, round head in the window looking right at me. I waited for him to come out, but he didn't move. I was already running a little late and wondered if we would make it in time for his appointment with the neurologist. Still, he didn't move. Rather than beep the horn, I got out to see why he wasn't coming. When my car door slammed shut, his body suddenly bounced to life and he jerked his head. I realized he had fallen asleep standing up, waiting for me.

I still took him to most of his doctor's appointments. But once things were a little more settled—with doctors that took his government insurance, actually asked him questions, listened to his answers, and really examined him—sometimes my parents took him. But I only let them do the easy ones: podiatrist, general practitioner, eye doctor. I wouldn't give up the neurologist.

Not long after that day, I was out of town when my mother took him to his appointment with a nutritionist, an expert in diabetic nutrition, to talk about his rising blood sugar. I had coached her on the phone before the appointment. I told her to make sure the nutritionist didn't yell at him for not losing weight and to explain to her that obesity is a side effect of both narcolepsy and fetal alcohol syndrome. That some of his nine medicines could elevate his blood glucose. That he didn't understand how to read nutrition labels and struggled with recipes. I reminded her that he gets nervous with doctors and anyone he perceives in a position of authority. I told her to not let them put him on insulin until we understood how it would affect his narcolepsy, until they talked to his neurologist. I reminded her of the baby she rescued all those years ago and that she wasn't done; she still needed to fight for him. My mother listened to me go on and on and promised to call me after the appointment.

"It didn't go well," were her first words when I answered the phone. *Shit.* I knew I should have taken him to the appointment.

"Bobby's fasting blood sugar was 544," my mother continued. Diabetes would be the latest in a long line of self-destructive attacks his body would wage against itself. "He's at risk of diabetic coma, aneurism, stroke, heart attack. Could happen at any time. He has to get his sugar down. He could die at any time, Kelly? Are you there?"

"Yes, I'm here. Keep going." I was taking notes as she was talking. I always took notes. I knew I would need them at some point. As I tried to keep up with her and write down the key words, my brain kept getting stuck on "he could die at any time."

"The doctor wants to prescribe insulin, one shot per day." I had been against putting him on insulin. He was already taking so many medications. Pills strong enough to keep him awake during the day; pills that control his cataplexy and electrical shocks that run through his body; the pill that is supposed to keep the hallucinations at bay; the pill he has to take to counteract the one that keeps him awake all day so he can sleep through the night; pills for his high cholesterol, triglycerides, and heartburn. How could one more drug be good for him?

"The doctor really thinks it will be okay. Our bodies make insulin already. It should make him feel better." I made a note to call his neurologist later to verify that insulin wouldn't make his narcolepsy worse.

"She is concerned that Bobby won't be able to manage this himself. He doesn't remember to take his medicine now. He can't forget his insulin. He also needs to change his diet and lose weight, which he doesn't seem able to do on his own." I don't argue with her. He didn't always remember. He needed to be reminded to take his medicines, to eat the right things, and he didn't always make the right decision. The diagnosis of his developmental disabilities as a result of fetal alcohol syndrome a few years ago helped us understand and accept why. Still, I was defensive when other people accused him of it.

"Kelly, she also mentioned a group home. Bobby broke down in the doctor's office as soon as she said it."

This is also when I broke down. *Group home.* I had trouble focusing on anything else my mother said after that. My throat closed off my words. I tried holding back my tears so I could finish the phone call, but I couldn't stop them. My tears fell, spotting my note pad.

"Mom, we're not putting him in a group home. He's thirty-seven years old."

"Kelly, it may be the only option."

"Well, it's going to be the last option. I'll stop every day on my way to work to give him his insulin shot." Before we hung up, we talked for a few more minutes about the details of when his prescription would be ready and whether or not my sister, Patti, an RN, could help set up home care.

I stopped trying to hold back my tears and I cried. My chest heaved with sobs I could no longer contain. Strange noises came from my throat. I was alone, and I didn't care what I looked like or sounded like. I let the cries come. I let the tears fall and my nose run. My mind drifted to Bobby, how upset he must have been; I wished I had been there at the doctor's office with him instead of my parents.

I called Bobby and we talked about what the doctor said. I told him we would do whatever we could. I told him he had to try harder, do better. He had to help me fight this. He promised to try harder, do better.

"We'll figure it out, Bob. We always do."

After we hung up, I lay down on the couch and closed my eyes. I tried to come up with a plan for this latest challenge, tried to think of the next thing I could do, the phone calls I needed to make.

Since Bobby came into my life thirty-six years ago, I had been trying to keep him alive and to help him find a place he can call home.

I had chased him all over Binghamton when he ran away at sixteen. When he came back, I still followed him. To East Canal Street, West Canal Street, our parents' home, Five Corners, Williams Street, Madison Street, Lenox Avenue, behind some bar on some street neither of us can remember, Canal Street again, Walnut Street, Florida Road, North Main Street, a friend's extra bedroom in Central Square, a friend's couch in North Syracuse, the John Milton Inn. Starting over again after the fire, searching and finding him over and over again, the jobs he had and lost, the testing, the doctors, the forms. All with one goal: to give him the life he deserves, the life he dreams of, his own corner of the world with a family and a home of his own. *A home of his own.*

...the silver lining

"It is never too late to be what you might have been."
– George Eliot

I'D LIKE YOU TO READ THIS BOOK." DR. MARSHA STOOD up from her armchair and walked to her desk on the other side of the room. She picked a book from the shelf and brought it back to me. "It's called *Perfect Daughters* by Robert J. Ackerman, PhD."

I took the book from her, looked at the cover, and read the tag line.

"It's for adult daughters of alcoholics." I looked up at Dr. Marsha, confused on why she would hand me this book. "That's not me."

"Why not? Your father is an alcoholic."

"No. He *was* an alcoholic. Was. He stopped drinking when I was seven or eight. For the rest of my childhood he was not." I knew I sounded defensive, but I felt strongly about this. God had performed a miracle when I was a little girl by saving my parents and their marriage. If he hadn't intervened, I would have been fatherless. I would have been a different person.

"Trust me on this, Kelly. These things you're struggling with are belief systems that took hold in your mind and soul in your earliest years. Read it and then tell me what you think."

I took the book home and read it in two days. I was shocked to find myself in the stories of the women included in those pages, women who were adult daughters of alcoholics. I had spent my life feeling different from other women but suddenly saw myself in their character profiles. They described behaviors and traits that I shared. If I please everyone, everyone will be happy; if I can control everything, I can keep my family from becoming upset; it is my fault, and I am to blame when trouble occurs; take care of others first; it is my responsibility to ensure that everyone in the family gets along with each other. The list was long, and not every item applied to me; however, I began to realize that my life and how I had designed it was based on patterns of behaviors and unintended childhood lessons that I had learned at some point. What I was discovering in those pages scared me, troubled me, and at the same time was a huge relief. I had always wondered and tortured myself with the same questions over and over again. *Why am I like I am? Why do I feel different than everyone else? Why didn't I want children? Will I regret it? Why did I pick the husband I did? Why does my family act the way they do? Do my brothers and sisters resent me? Why am I the peacekeeper? Why did I take other people's lives and decisions so personally? Why did it impact me so deeply?*

The book also discussed self-condemnation and the destructive habit I had of judging myself without mercy. I had plenty of acceptance and kindness for the people around me, no matter what they did, but when it came to me, I was demanding and unforgiving. As Dr. Ackerman explained, "Self-condemnation results from never feeling that you are good enough and that whatever goes wrong is your fault."

Dr. Marsha was right, as usual. This book explained it all. I never would have described or categorized myself as an "adult daughter of an alcoholic." Never. My father was the best man I knew. I felt like I was betraying him by even considering it. Yes, he had stopped drinking when I was seven or eight. But the damage had been done.

This book also outlined different personality types. While not every type of adult daughter applied to me, it was sobering how many of them I did identify with. Ackerman described "the achiever" as someone who had difficulty relaxing, couldn't express their feelings, was validated only externally, and feared failure. Then there was "the other-directed one" who was overly controlled by others, tense, anxious, and over-reactive. That was definitely me. "The conflict avoider" tended to find herself in the middle of other people's problems, willing to help everyone with their problems as they avoided their own, a people-pleaser who will do anything to avoid her own problems or difficult feelings. Yup, me again. Dr. Marsha's face flashed before my eyes. Then there was "the hyper-mature" character that tended to be too serious, had difficulty expressing emotions, constantly needed control, had stress related illnesses (migraines), was fearful, driven, and blamed themselves too much.

I remembered my first migraine headache. I think I was about eight or nine years old. I don't remember that day as anything out of the ordinary. I only remembered sitting at the kitchen counter in my bathrobe trying to explain the overwhelming pain to my mother, pain so overwhelming that the only way through it was to lie down on the couch and wait for the nausea to subside. She brought me a cold washcloth and laid it over my eyes to block out all light. I continue to experience migraines to this day.

After reading *Perfect Daughters*, I could not deny that I was impacted by my early childhood, the dynamics of my family, and my parents' relationship. I did not believe I was an extreme case of any of those types of adult daughters. Not all of them applied to me, probably because things turned for the better while I was still fairly young. However, the threads in those personalities of fear, self-blame, difficulty defining my feelings, and being overly controlled by what others were doing or not doing were exactly what Dr. Marsha had been helping me to see for myself during all of our excruciating sessions together.

Yet in those pages, I also found a silver lining. I hadn't developed only negative behaviors. I had also developed the skills and strengths that had made me successful in most areas of my life. I had also learned along the way how to negotiate conflict and had become very good at problem solving. I was calm and steadfast in a crisis and had developed enviable leadership skills. I could take care of myself. I was strong and independent. This same childhood of mine had resulted in a host of characteristics that would sustain me, cause me to thrive in my career, and give me the empathy and compassion that drove me to want to change the world. Those were the things I needed to appreciate and focus on. I needed to nourish those qualities within me that were good and let go of the weeds that were trying to choke out the flowers.

For me, I could finally see that all of it boiled down to this: somewhere along the line, I had become convinced that I was not okay, because if I was okay, these problems wouldn't exist in my family. My father wouldn't drink and be unhappy, and my mother wouldn't be sad and want to leave. If I were okay, then they would be okay. If I could keep the peace, then my entire world would not fall apart. I took on this tremendous burden and responsibility for six other people individually and as a unit. If I was a good girl and cleaned the house, did the gardening, did the housework, maybe then my mother would be happier. If I agreed with both Shelly and Patti and didn't pick sides, then they wouldn't fight. If I could take on some of the burden of Bobby, then my mother wouldn't resent him so much. If I could make my father smile, then maybe he wouldn't leave us. *God, how did this happen without anyone knowing it? Without me realizing it?* I had developed the belief at my core that I was not okay as I was. I was convinced I'd be rejected if people saw the real me.

Talking about *Perfect Daughters* with Dr. Marsha after I read it was one of my last sessions alone with her. It had been more than two years since we started therapy. I was grateful for all I had learned about myself, and I knew it would take time for me to change.

"Your anger, sadness, and determination are what will drive that change," Dr. Marsha said.

If I didn't commit to this change, I would keep repeating the behavior with a new husband, a new job, a new family, or new city. Wherever I go, there I am.

However, I still struggled with one thing. The love I felt for my family was real. My heart was pure and full of love when I helped others. My desire to help them and do whatever I could to make them happy was authentic. Perhaps it was exploited by my other dysfunctional needs, but the love was real. All of these "family of origin" things happened before Bobby showed up in my life. Maybe all of these things happened to me on purpose. Maybe God knew all along that this eight-year-old girl would be poised and ready to love this ten-month-old baby who would need her more than anyone ever had. I knew I would never apologize for my compassion, for my love of family and others, my desire to serve my community and people in need. I would never apologize for the relationship I had with my brother, Bobby. And I certainly would never apologize for being relentless in my determination to help him find his home on this earth. Maybe *this* is exactly how I was supposed to be.

SOMEDAY

I PULLED INTO BOBBY'S DRIVEWAY BUT DIDN'T SEE HIM. I tried calling his cell again. No answer. I had already called twice after I left work and was on my way to his place. He knew I was stopping by. Why hadn't he answered? I got out of my car and stepped inside the garage. His bike was there. The lawn mower was there. That was a good sign. He wasn't working at one of his clients' houses. He had asked me to print business cards on my computer a few years ago so he could look for work in his neighborhood. "Able to provide: lawn mowing; weeding; snow shoveling; clean up and organization of your garage, basement, or shed; debris removal; and general labor in the yard or home."

I walked up the stairs to his apartment over the garage. I knocked on the door, loud, calling his name. Fortunately, Chris, the ninety-seven-year-old man who lived in the house attached to the garage, couldn't hear very well. He owned the house and the apartment Bobby lived in. Bobby had lived there since the fire four years before, the longest he'd lived anywhere since he ran away from home at sixteen. Bobby took care of the yard and the shoveling. When Bobby ordered take-out, he ordered extra chicken wings because they were Chris' favorite. If he

cooked, he'd make a plate of lasagna or chicken and potatoes or whatever he was having for dinner and took it downstairs to eat with him.
Chris left his newspaper on Bobby's step after he was done with it.
He worried if Bobby wasn't home by a decent hour. One Friday night
after work, I had talked to Bobby when he was planning supper.

"What's for dinner tonight, Bob?"

"It's Friday. Poultry night."

"Oh, are you getting one of those roasted chickens from the grocery store?"

"No. Fish fry." My silence must have been obvious.

"Isn't fish poultry?" he asked.

"No, Bob, fish is fish."

Although we talked on the phone daily, I never liked to go more
than a week without actually seeing him. I would stop by his house
once a week or so to pick up bills that needed to be paid, food stamp
forms that needed to be filled out, or a Medicaid recertification that
was due. I checked his pill bottles to make sure he had refills left or
to find prescriptions that needed to be called in. He worked Tues-
days and Fridays at the convenience store, so I usually didn't stop
on those days.

I knocked on his door, louder, and called his name, again. I hated
to open the door, unsure of what I'd find. Perhaps him naked, just
out of the shower or lying on the floor unconscious, bloodied, and
bruised from a fall. But I had no choice. I had to go in. He needed
cash for the Country Music Throwdown on Sunday, and I was going
out of town for the weekend. He had been planning this for months.
It was an all-day event at the fairgrounds with a list of country
music bands and singers. He had me set aside seventy dollars for
food, a T-shirt, and anything else that caught his eye.

I opened the door, yelling his name while averting my eyes, just in case. When he didn't answer, I let my eyes open and looked around his apartment. The bathroom door was open, his purple shower curtain was closed, no sign of him except for a radio playing. I looked toward the bedroom and didn't see his feet on the bed, so I stepped in. Fan on. TV on. No Bob. The living room was empty; that TV was also on. He was always forgetting to turn things off. There was a checklist that hung by his door. He was supposed to read through it before he left. *Make sure stove and oven are off. Turn off lights. Turn off faucets.* His computer room was empty. I looked in the kitchen, empty except for a sink full of dirty dishes. I left the cash on his hutch, picked up his cable and electric bill, walked out, and closed the door behind me.

Downstairs, I looked out the back window; the yard was empty. I walked out of the garage and headed to my car. I decided to take one last look and checked out the side yard. At the edge of the driveway, I peeked around the house. I saw a blue shirt on the bench swing.

"Bob?" The blue shirt moved. I stepped up on the retaining wall and walked toward him. "What're you doing?" He sat up, took his headphones off, blinked his eyes, and yawned. "I've been calling you. Did you forget I was coming by?"

"I didn't forget. I just sat here to cool off. I must have fallen asleep."

The sun was still warm, and the lawn was freshly mowed. His neighborhood was quiet. Bobby was quiet, still trying to wake up.

"Do you feel okay?" I asked.

I sat next to him on the swing.

"You don't look good," I told him. He wore his life in the dark circles under his eyes, the fading purple bruises from last week's fall, his bad teeth—the spaces where teeth used to be, now gone for good—the extra pounds that made him uncomfortable. His short hair showed the slightest signs of gray, the receding edges carved out two crescent moon shapes on both sides of his widow's peak. He was no longer the ten-month-old baby in need of rescue. He was more than a diagnosis or a disease or a disability. I was no longer the eight-year-old girl who needed to fix everything and everyone in order to keep her home intact. He was my home.

"I'm all right."

"Okay. Remember, I'm going away for the weekend."

"Don't forget those other tickets I want. Jason Aldean. They go on sale at 9:00 a.m. Saturday morning."

"I'll bring my laptop. I'm sure the hotel has Wi-Fi." He had been waiting months for those tickets to go on sale. That concert was in August. "Have fun on Sunday at the Throwdown. Mom and Dad are going to take you, and then Kevin and I will be back in time to pick you up when it's over. Are you sure you're okay? Do you need anything?"

"No, I'm good. I'm gonna get up and get something to eat. Hey, did you see that house on the corner? It's for sale."

"Yeah, I saw it. Looks like it would be perfect for you."

"Yeah, someday..."

I stood up and turned around to look at him before I said good-bye, wishing I could give him the life *he* dreamt of, knowing that I couldn't, knowing as long as he kept dreaming, I'd keep doing what I could to get him as close as possible. The merry-go-round kept moving, spinning faster and faster, but the quest to get him on the ride was no longer important. There were times I thought about giving up, feeling the futility of it all, but that thought left as quickly as it came, floating through my mind like the silky, white insides of the milkweed. I wouldn't give up because he never had.

"Gotta run, Bob. I'll see you later. Love you."

"Love you too."

A few months later on a Saturday morning, I drove to Bobby's place to pick him up. He was coming with me to run a few errands, and I was taking him to pick out new frames and lenses with the eye doctor. I called him when I was on my way, just to make sure he was awake, dressed, and ready to go. I turned onto his street. He was standing at the end of his driveway holding a bag of tomatoes for me. They were from his landlord's garden; he had been trying to get them to me for more than a week. He held something else in his other hand. I pulled in and saw that it was a dark pink rose he had picked from the thorny bushes that lined his driveway. I rolled down my window, and without words or ceremony he handed me the flower. And without words or ceremony, I accepted it. I held it in my hand while he got in the car, and we drove away. I held it, treasured it, until I placed it in a small crystal vase at home. I was not surprised by that unexpected gift, on that ordinary Saturday, because I had learned, that's just the way he is.

EPILOGUE

BOBBY AND I CONTINUE TO NAVIGATE OUR CORNER of the world together. He still works ten-to-fifteen hours per week at the convenience store cleaning the car wash bays and doing other maintenance. They've been good to him for the past ten years and make him feel important. He stayed in that last apartment for five years but had to move when his landlord died. For now, he shares a house with his daughter, his ex-wife, and her new husband—an unconventional set up that has worked well for him. His doctors continue to fine-tune his medications in order to battle his narcolepsy symptoms in the most effective way they can. Bobby finds contentment and joy in the simple pleasures of life: his favorite music, a good meal, collecting treasures, and spending time with his family. Although life is hard and unfair, he gets up every day and keeps going, riding the bus, working when he can. Occasionally, we still have challenges that shake us both.

My phone rang while I was at work on a recent Friday afternoon.

"Hey. What's up?" I said. It was unusual for Bobby to call me this early, so I was surprised to hear his voice.

"What hospital do I go to?" Bobby asked.

"What do you mean?"

"You know, what emergency room should I go to?"

"Bob. Start from the beginning. What's going on? Where are you?"

"I just got off the bus, and I can't breathe. My chest hurts. I'm walking to Upstate Hospital."

"Where are you exactly? Call Uber or a cab or an ambulance. Don't walk if you can't breathe."

"I'm almost there now."

"Okay. Get yourself there and checked in. Call me and let me know what's happening."

I hung up the phone and sent out a group text to my sisters and brother to let them know Bobby was on his way to the emergency room. I called my mother as well.

I wouldn't be able to focus on anything else until I knew Bobby was okay. He struggled with the same chronic lung disease that his biological father had, and I knew from past experience that pneumonia had probably settled in his lungs.

As I mentioned at the beginning of this story, life is messy and often takes unexpected turns. Kevin and I worked very hard to save our marriage, and just when I thought we had made it through, our marriage ended. In 2014, I found myself alone in our dream home, lost and struggling with the grief and regret that follows divorce. When my company gave me the opportunity, I moved to Boston for almost two years, trying to outrun my loneliness and sadness.

Our divorce was hard on Bobby. A few months after Kevin moved out, Bobby and I were on the phone for one of our checking-in-at-the-end-of-the-day conversations. I was actually talking about this book and the struggle to get it published. He said he had questions "for the book," questions he'd like to ask me. He was being coy and indirect, so I knew something was up.

"What? What would you ask me?" I asked.

"Did Kevin leave you because of me?" My heart stopped.

"No, of course not."

"You know, because you have to spend so much time on me."

"Bob, I promise you, Kevin leaving me has nothing to do with you."

"Oh, okay. I've been wondering."

He was still that sweet little boy I fell in love with the first time I saw him.

Even though helping Bobby had been all-consuming at times, almost like a second job, I know it had nothing to do with the demise of my marriage. Kevin still takes Bobby to hockey games and Christmas shopping every year and continues to show up for important events in his life.

I found love again in the most unexpected and surprising way and chased it all the way to San Diego, California. Living so far away from home has been challenging at times, especially when Bobby was on his way to the hospital on a Friday afternoon.

Bobby called my sister, Patti, from the ER, scared and sobbing. The doctor didn't think he had pneumonia but was concerned he could have a blood clot in his lungs. I had left work and was driving home when my sister called me. As she gave me the latest news on Bobby, I reminded her: "Make sure you speak up. You know how they treat Medicaid patients. You have to be pushy with the doctors. Make sure they know about his narcolepsy and all the medicine he takes. Call me as soon as you hear anything."

I managed to choke out, "Tell Bobby I love him," before I hung up. I cried all the way home and kept my phone with me the rest of the night. I tried not to think about losing him. I couldn't imagine my world without him in it. Patti stayed with Bobby for hours while they tried to figure out what was happening with his health.

With the long distance between us now, Bobby and I have had to get creative and put some new systems in place. We've made it work. He has a solid support system of friends and family who can give him a ride to the grocery store or the doctor's office. Even though we knew we would miss each other terribly, Bobby gave me his blessing and told me he thought I needed this move in order to be happy. We talk on the phone every day and use FaceTime a lot. I still pay his bills and manage his money, and we visit each other as often as possible. We even managed to fulfill one of his lifelong dreams together when I took him to Nashville. I know that Bobby and I will find ourselves in the same place again; we are soul mates. It is our destiny.

The doctors did not find a blood clot in Bobby's lungs that Friday, and by the next morning, they had decided to treat him for pneumonia. I breathed another sigh of relief, at least for now.

This story, the story of Bobby and me, was always about home. Bobby was suddenly removed from his birth home at ten months old and has spent the rest of his life searching for and wanting desperately to have his own home, getting close at times but never quite attaining it. For Bobby, home is tangible: a place and structure constructed of a dining room, a garage, a yard.

I've learned from Bobby and my work with Dr. Marsha that I

have also been on a quest for home. But for me, home is abstract: an ideal constructed of the people I love. My quest has been to keep those people intact, safe, cared for, and stable. Only then could my home be at peace.

I know now that my home cannot be built on the premise that everyone I love remains in a perfect state of happiness, safety, success, and peace. We must face each other's imperfections, sicknesses, labels, and messes. We own each other's mistakes, regrets, failures, and bad decisions. But we celebrate it all: our faith in God, good health, meals together, and laughter.

I know now that it was never my responsibility to be the keeper of peace, keeper of emotions, keeper of our home or baby brothers. I am just here, in my corner of the world. Here to love my parents, my brothers and sisters, my nieces and nephews, and anyone else who joins us on this journey. It was never my job to rescue or fix Bobby. It was my destiny to love him—just the way he is.

This is enough for me. This is my home. This is all there is.

ACKNOWLEDGMENTS

To God: Thank you for your favor and unmerited grace that surrounds me and allows me to live the life I have. Thank you for the parents you gave me and for rescuing my family on that warm July night in 1975 at Camp Aldersgate so that we could be there for Bobby when he needed us.

To my parents: Thank you for your unconditional love, unwavering faith, and for always believing in me.

To my brother, Tim, and my sisters, Shelly and Patti, their partners, and their kids whom they've unselfishly shared with me: Thank you for being my family and for putting up with me. You are my home.

To Craig: You have been the biggest surprise of my life. I can't wait to see where our story takes us. Thank you for your support as I've worked to share this story with the world.

To the Staff and Instructors of the YMCA's Downtown Writers Center in Syracuse, New York: Thank you for giving me permission to write, confidence in my abilities, and the skills to back it up.

To Crystal, Eric, Ermine, Kathy, and Pete: Thank you for listening. I will never forget our time together, and I'm so happy that writing this story brought you into my life for a season. To Linda Lowen: Thank you for going above and beyond and for believing in my story.

To Kevin: You were at my side for the toughest parts of this story and were there as I relived all of it again through writing about it. Although we are not side-by-side anymore, the way you've always been there for Bobby means everything to me. Thank you.

To Bobby: You've inspired me to see the world differently. You've taught me that it is in fact the simple things in life that can make a person happy—family, friends, good music, good food. You've taught me that when you truly love someone you allow them to live the life God has planned for them, not the life you imagined for them. You've also shown me that even though we may not always get the life we dream of, it is still a life that is ours and happiness can be found. You've shown me how to find the treasure, not only in the small, simple things in life, but the treasure that is all around. You've let me see the treasure in people—the treasure in you. Thank you for it all.

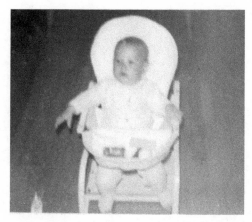

Bouncy-Seat Bobby: Not long after he came to live with us.

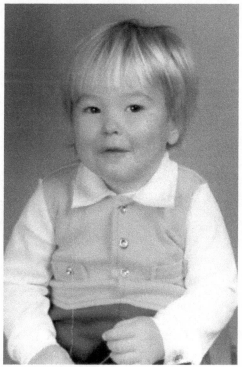

Eighteen months: Right around the time Bobby taught himself to whistle.

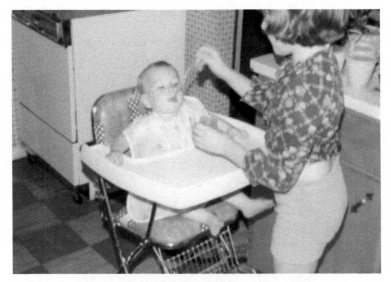

1976: I love this picture of us—seems so fitting now.

1977: Our backyard—Bobby's favorite place to play.
His sand pile sat behind that shed.

*Asleep standing up: At the clothesline holding his
"nigh, nigh" and sucking his thumb.*

Four or five years old: His eyes seem to tell so much beyond his years.

Kindergarten: Looking adorable and mischievous.

First grade: Suddenly a little boy.

*Eighth or ninth grade: Not too long before
Bobby ran away from home.*

2017: Still one of my favorite people to hang out with—we went to the rodeo to celebrate Bobby's birthday during his first trip to California.